Praise for *The Climb to Investment Excellence*

"Institutional pools of capital are among the least understood and most important investment pools in the world. After nearly four decades in the trenches, half as a direct investor and half on the buy side of the buy side, Ana deeply understands the investment process employed by institutional Chief Investment Officers. In *The Climb to Investment Excellence*, she shares both the building blocks of how it all works and her unique insights into each aspect of the process. Her work is a must read for those seeking to understand how this opaque corner of the investment world operates."

—Ted Seides, Capital Allocators

"Ana Marshall's book is required reading for anyone managing money or anyone looking to learn how to become an excellent investor—or simply looking to be inspired by the idea of investing well and doing good with it. Ana does a great job in distilling complex subjects into actionable decisions, as well as provide valuable insights on themes not normally covered well in books on investing—the importance of relationships with boards, committees, investment managers, and her team cannot be understated."

—James Manyika, SVP Google-Alphabet,
Chair and director emeritus, McKinsey Global Institute

"Ana demystifies long-term investing by sharing both her direct experience and the intelligence she has gathered over the last 20 years as a successful practitioner. This book is essential reading for anyone involved in a voluntary or professional basis managing long term pools of capital. There is a chapter for everyone: trustees, board/committee members, fellow CIOs and their team members. Also highly recommended reading for General Partners and investment managers who manage non-profit money, it provides deep insight into the governance and investment practices of their investors enabling both to build stronger partnerships."

—Sandra Robertson, CEO and CIO Oxford
University Endowment Management

"This is a 'must read' book for investment committee and board members responsible for overseeing large sums of capital and setting the standards to achieve excellence. Very few investment professionals have been as thoughtful about the investment process as Ana. Add to that her innate ability to join the dots from disparate pieces of information and data, and you have the winning performance she has demonstrated."

—Boon Hwee Koh, Board Member GIC
and Singapore Stock Exchange

THE CLIMB TO INVESTMENT EXCELLENCE

THE CLIMB TO INVESTMENT EXCELLENCE

A PRACTITIONER'S GUIDE TO BUILDING EXCEPTIONAL PORTFOLIOS AND TEAMS

ANA MARSHALL, CFA

WILEY

Published by John Wiley & Sons, Inc., Hoboken, New Jersey.
Published simultaneously in Canada.

For general information on our other products and services or for technical support, please contact our Customer Care Department within the United States at (800) 762-2974, outside the United States at (317) 572-3993 or fax (317) 572-4002.

Wiley also publishes its books in a variety of electronic formats. Some content that appears in print may not be available in electronic formats. For more information about Wiley products, visit our web site at www.wiley.com.

Library of Congress Cataloging-in-Publication Data
Names: Marshall, Ana, author.
Title: The climb to investment excellence: a practitioner's guide to
   building exceptional portfolios and team / Ana Marshall.
Description: Hoboken, New Jersey : Wiley, [2024]
Identifiers: LCCN 2023024882 (print) | LCCN 2023024883 (ebook) | ISBN
   9781394206698 (hardback) | ISBN 9781394206711 (adobe pdf) | ISBN
   9781394206704 (epub)
Subjects: LCSH: Investments. | Portfolio management.
Classification: LCC HG4521 .M219 2023 (print) | LCC HG4521 (ebook) | DDC
   332.6—dc23/eng/20230721
LC record available at https://lccn.loc.gov/2023024882
LC ebook record available at https://lccn.loc.gov/2023024883

Cover Design: Wiley
Cover Image: © Overearth/Getty Images

SKY10055338_091523

With gratitude to my incredible husband and kids —
my expedition team for life

Contents

Prologue

Somewhere between the bottom of the climb and the summit is the answer to the mystery of why we climb.

—*Greg Child*[1]

Climbing a technically difficult mountain like Everest, K2, or Denali is similar to creating an excellent investment portfolio. Being excellent at investing is hard. Climbing to the top of Everest or Kilimanjaro is hard. Thousands of alpinists make the attempt to reach the summit every year, both in mountain climbing and investing. Many fail to move successfully from base camp through to the summit.

This book is a handbook to help anyone with a fiduciary responsibility for overseeing or managing significant sums of capital. Many books on investing suggest there is one mountain worth climbing, one right way to do it, one definitive answer. I would argue that similar to ascending to a mountain summit, there is no single route or definitive guide to the top. Every organization has different goals, operating requirements, and priorities.

A long-term investment strategy provides a road map that rarely is able to anticipate the cyclical and secular hazards in capital markets and the economy. There are limitations to any climbing plan, and they must be overcome to reach the top. The art of investing is how investors execute the plan in spite of the challenges on the way to the summit. My goal in this book is to give you the tools to construct an excellent investment program along with the courage to adapt plans to reach the summit.

Alpinism is similar to investing in that it is the interplay between the technical skills and endurance of the climber/investor and the conditions

---

[1] Greg Child, from an interview in Jonathan Waterman, "The Natural: Greg Child," in Jonathan Waterman, ed., *Cloud Dancers: Portraits of North American Mountaineers* (Golden, CO: AAC Press, 1993), 280.

of the mountain/market that result in a successful summit. Before heading into any climb, having well-honed expert technique, the right climbing gear, and knowing the routes to ascend are essential requirements for a successful climb. However, skill and a plan are not enough. To climb successfully to the summit, one must be able to adapt quickly and be able to navigate under unexpected changes in the environment. The mountains and markets are full of cautionary tales. The main goal, besides success in making it to the top, is survival.

Investing and climbing involve repetitive processes of thinking, problem solving, and executing. Thinking outside traditional frameworks, solving problems, and then executing the solution a hundred times a year, and thousands of times in a career is how to build muscle memory. It takes years of practice and living at altitudes where the air is thin and ever changing, to be able to ascend and not succumb to the wear and tear of the climb.

Importantly, one never climbs alone. There is a team that works together to improve the probability of making it to the summit. The chief investment officer (CIO) is the expedition guide charged with the responsibility of making sure the team makes it to the summit. As with any intensive sport, discipline, hard work, and practice are essential. The leader must take a group of competitive individuals and form a team that is attuned to the tempo of the mountain and the hazards of storms.

During my career I have identified attractive investment strategies only to be faced with unanticipated hazards. From my early days as a high-yield credit analyst, I learned fundamental value didn't protect downside in the face of the Drexel Burnham Lambert bankruptcy in 1990. During the 1990s, I was recruited to summit a new, technically challenging peak: investing in emerging markets. I soon realized that company fundamentals could be blown off course by exogenous factors (currency devaluations, political coups, etc.) that suddenly appeared and turned into full-blown storms called the Tequila Crisis of 1994, the Asian Crisis of 1997, and the Russia Crisis of 1998.

Wanting the challenges of a new adventure, I set my sights on a new summit, managing global equities, only to be caught in a blinding snowstorm when the internet bubble popped in 2000–2001. Once adjusted to the new environment, the strategic plan was, yet again, taken off course by 9/11 in 2001 and the spectacular corporate frauds of Enron and WorldCom in 2003. Successfully managing client portfolios during difficult times increased my resilience and ingrained a determination to survive whatever hazards came my way.

In 2004, I was asked to join a new expedition team to climb the most challenging mountain of my career. Laurie Hoagland[2] was assembling a new expedition team to take the $4 billion Hewlett Foundation endowment to new heights. He recognized a fellow investor and believed my skills in global fixed income and equities would be of great use as we built the Hewlett diversified portfolio. I lacked certain technical skills necessary to get to first camp. He took the time to teach me the importance of governance, clear objectives, asset allocation, and developing a policy portfolio. His expectations of me were clear from the start. He expected me to take over as the expedition team leader somewhere between first and second camp. Even this plan didn't go as anticipated. As it turns out, there was so much work involved in ensuring that the investment program could weather the storm, that he and I, along with the rest of the team, knew we would be stronger staying on course together. Very little went according to our expectations. When the Great Financial Crisis (GFC) hit in 2008, the storm was clearly surrounding us. This was the moment in which Laurie and I had the critical conversation of what it would take to lead the portfolio and team to safer ground. We knew in theory what it would take to recover strength and trek on. It took grit and determination to keep moving with little visibility ahead.

Being successful in investing requires a mix of theory, practice, and luck. If the terrain and ice conditions didn't change, or if the sun, wind, or snow were perfectly predictable, then machines could do what we do. Combining theory and practice ensures that the climbing, or investing, team has the chance to change path, slow or accelerate the pace, and it improves the chance of making it to the top. The alternative is to wait out the elements as they hit parts of the endowment portfolio.

Some people believe machines can do what we do, but I would argue that investor behavior is difficult to predict in the moment. This is the reason why, despite excellent mathematical models, expected volatility still differs from realized volatility. However, we are in the early stages of knowing the capabilities of artificial intelligence, and some degree technological disruption of the investment office is likely to occur over the coming decade.

This book offers a practical guide to things any investor or anyone serving as a fiduciary (on a board or investment committee) should consider before deciding on the objective of an investment program.

---

[2] Laurence "Laurie" Hoagland was a legendary investor and mentor who understood that forming the expedition team was the key to success. He was the first CIO of Stanford Management Company and a lifelong friend of the Hewlett family.

The practical advice combines 18 years as a GP/investor and 18 years as an allocator of capital. It sets out the skills needed to have a high probability of succeeding on the ascent, and also takes into account the luck and the resilience investors must have to climb to the summit in the investing world. It doesn't have magic formulas, nor quick fixes, because investing takes hard work and the ability to think quickly and adapt to a changing environment. However, it does provide easy-to-reference lists of things to consider when faced with decision points and gives ideas on how to adapt plans in order to survive and continue the climb when conditions force a change and things go wrong.

The book has three sections.

The first is focused on preparing for the climb and reaching base camp. Think of this part as the chapters on the logistics that will be crucial to make sure you and your team have a successful expedition. These are the chapters where the organization[3] identifies the summit for the expedition, responsibilities are clarified, and the team has the time to adjust to the altitude (the headaches, the pressure, etc.). You need to make sure everyone involved in the expedition, including the client, the board, and the investment committee, is clear on the goal, the tools, and the capability of the team. The pacing of the expedition is established, and the decision of whether the team will carry heavy packs or lightweight packs is made. Reaching base camp and setting asset allocation policy can only be done after the logistics have been put into place and the pack lists have been checked.

The second part of the book has the practical aspects of the ascent from first camp through third camp. These chapters cover the primary responsibilities of managing an investment portfolio. Developing the policy portfolio serves as the first resting spot after leaving base camp. Between first camp and second camp, the team implements the policy portfolio, adapting and using the portfolio management tools available to navigate ever-changing conditions. Moving from second camp to third camp, manager selection and diligence offer up different types of hazards.

The third part of the book is the final push to the summit, where leadership and endurance play a critical role. This is the most dangerous part of the climb, and also where most teams fail. This part provides tips

---

[3]Throughout the book I refer to organization or institution because that is my point of reference. The lessons and tools can apply to family offices and multi-client fiduciaries. I also refer to the chief investment officer (CIO) as the team leader but recognize in some organizations the title of the expedition leader may differ.

on setting best practices for your investment program in managing all of the members of the climbing team: the investment team, the board, the managers, and the other climbers on the mountain. Creating team culture and inspiring the team as the air thins and the ice storms come, more often than not, are just a few of the challenges in managing highly competitive and ambitious climbers. Finally, in reaching the summit, an investor is forced to look within to one's competitive edge in order to find the way home.

There are three underlying themes woven into every chapter because they are always top of mind for a successful alpinist. The first is having a well-thought-out strategy or plan as to how the team will ascend. The second is risk management because every decision must weigh the promise of progress against the risk to the team and the mission. The third is trust because the alpinist needs to be someone who is deeply trusted by their expedition team and the other climbers on the mountain. The organizations we work for trust that we will be successful ascending to the summit, taking only as much risk as necessary to achieve our objective.

Finally, a word of encouragement as you attempt the climb. It takes years to prepare physically and mentally to be able to ascend to the summit. Many of the greatest alpinists spent years training as porters, learning from experienced alpinist teams. As porters who prepare the route and carry supplies, they spent untold hours observing the mistakes made along the way, analyzing the paths chosen, and the difficult in-the-moment decisions made. I spent the first nine years of my career as an analyst (porter) learning from great investors around me. I observed how teams were formed and how they fell apart. I learned that having tools and skills is not enough. I learned to identify courageous, resilient leaders in the face of adversity and also the joy that comes from taking advantage of clear skies and cheering on the team as they triumph over unforeseen obstacles.

Part I

BASE CAMP – THE ADVENTURE BEGINS

Preparing for Base Camp

1

Identifying the Summit

Attempting to climb Everest is an intrinsically irrational act – a triumph of desire over sensibility.

—John Krakauer, *Into Thin Air*[1]

Whether you are starting a new investment office, creating an investment strategy for a new client, or the investment office has existed for decades, it is important to ensure that the objective of the investment program is clear. Different types of organizations have different priorities and objectives. Almost every organization has conflicting priorities between the staff and investment committee (IC) and board, regardless of whether the organization is a family office, pension fund, endowment, or foundation. There are several areas where the board and IC need to reconcile different priorities to develop a clear and cohesive role of the investment program in funding the needs of the organization in the near and long term. Table 1.1 sets out four areas to consider.

Just because Everest is there doesn't mean that this is the right goal and that investors have to climb that particular summit. How complex one makes a portfolio is a choice, just like choosing a less difficult mountain to climb. The portfolio should not be too complex relative to the needs of the organization or too difficult to implement, taking into account the skill set and resources of the investment team.

---

[1] John Krakauer, *Into Thin Air* (New York: Knopf Doubleday Publishing Group, 1998).

Table 1.1

Considerations for Identifying the Summit
1. Setting the investment objective
2. Understanding constraints and payout needs
3. Agreement on risk tolerance
4. Setting the time horizon

Source: The William and Flora Hewlett Foundation.

Managing a diversified institutional portfolio that delivers consistently superior returns is hard. Unless an investment program is staffed with the technical skills and access to top investment managers, perhaps choosing a portfolio with low cost and liquid funds with less complexity may be the best option. The goal is to reach the summit and have an excellent investment program. The view from the summit is worthwhile, no matter what mountain one has chosen to climb.

Setting the Investment Objective

Since the investment program is designed to achieve the investment objective, it really is worth having a fresh conversation to ensure the organization has a clear understanding of the investment program objective formally set in the investment policy statement (IPS) approved by the board of directors. The IPS serves as the North Star for strategic asset allocation, risk management, and liquidity management of an institutional portfolio. It goes without saying that the foremost responsibility of the CIO is to provide liquidity to fund the obligations of the organization and to achieve the investment objective.

On occasion, institutions choose to modify the IPS to reflect changes in spending needs or other priorities. It is natural to expect institutions to shift priorities over time as new leadership takes on new strategic direction, and the natural rotation of members of the board surfaces new ideas. The CIO is responsible for ensuring that the latest version of the IPS reflects current priorities, because it is the clearest directive of the strategy that must be implemented to achieve the objectives of the institution.

Defining what success looks like is key. Despite having a clearly stated IPS, a CIO should not assume that a successful investment program will be judged in the same way by the board and by the institution. Agreement between the board and the IC, and clear communication with the CIO on the criteria used to judge success of the investment program are critical to long-term achievement of the goal. The CIO needs to understand whether the IC thinks of returns in absolute terms, or in relative terms, and whether returns will be judged relative to the benchmark or relative to a narrow set of peer organizations.

Importantly, defining success does not have to be complicated. In fact, the simpler and clearer it is, the better for all concerned. Think of an IPS as the identification of the summit, and the packs and loads the expedition will have to carry to the summit. The organization can choose to burden the expedition with heavy packs (restrictions) or encourage lightweight packs to encourage adaptability. Importantly, the IPS reflects the key priorities of the organization. Below I provide examples of an IPS from three distinct organizations with different priorities.

At Hewlett Foundation, the priority is to preserve the spending power of the endowment in perpetuity by focusing on growing the endowment and on disciplined spending:

> The Hewlett Foundation seeks to maintain or grow current asset size and spending power in real (inflation-adjusted) terms with risk at a level appropriate to the Foundation's program objectives. There may be occasions when financial markets are down in ways that could require spending reductions in order to meet this objective. The board will ordinarily reduce spending in a downturn in order to mitigate the potential reduction in the Foundation's real value. (For purposes of this policy statement, a downturn is defined as negative return before payout in a calendar year.) Upon a vote of the majority of the board, the board may choose not to reduce spending in exceptional circumstances.

Some may consider defining a downturn as simply as "a negative return in a calendar year" as being too short-term oriented. Every institution is different. From experience, our conversations with the Hewlett board have focused on high sensitivity to a material decline in the value of the investment portfolio. Hewlett's spending policy is to spend between 4.75% and 5.75% of the foundation's assets averaged over a three-year period. As a pragmatic matter, we usually use 5.1%. If the investment return of the Hewlett endowment in any calendar year is negative, our plan calls for budgeting an amount equal to 5.1% of the estimated assets at the end of that year (i.e., without three-year smoothing).

At Skoll Foundation, an organization where the donor is actively increasing funding, the priority is to have the endowment portfolio investments aligned with the mission:

> The Skoll Foundation seeks to use all its resources to further its mission which provides the overarching framework for management of its financial capital. The Foundation acknowledges that the management of its assets must include the integration of prudent financial practices with principles of environmental stewardship, inclusive economic growth, and overall alignment with the Foundation's mission. In service of this mission the specific investment goals of the Foundation are: (1) to generate income necessary to fund the Foundation's spending on grants, program related investments and operations over the long-term; (2) to grow the real value of the Foundation's financial assets over the long term with consideration of the Foundation's spending levels; and, (3) to seek investments in funds and companies whose practices and products further advance the Foundation's mission while avoiding investments in entities whose actions work counter to the Foundation's mission, unless the Foundation determines that engagement with such entities will result in developments that may benefit relevant communities.

At an (undisclosed) family office, the objective is compounding of the endowment and diversification from the entrepreneur's primary source of wealth:

> The objective of the investment program is to generate superior risk-adjusted returns to compound the investment portfolio, taking into account the risk tolerance of the family. The investment program should over time provide diversification away from the core business of the family. The investment program is intended to provide liquidity to support the family's philanthropic efforts and payout needs as approved by the board.

While a CIO aims to construct an optimal investment portfolio, the reality is that there are many factors that must be considered in setting the IPS such as those listed in Table 1.2.

Understanding Constraints and Payout

The IPS and the answers to the questions referenced in Table 1.2 inform the constraints the CIO must incorporate in developing the policy portfolio. Whether an organization is expected to exist in perpetuity or

Table 1.2

Factors to Consider in IPS
• Is the organization perpetual or spend-down?
• Are there additional contributions of capital into the endowment?
• What is the payout expected from the endowment portfolio?
• Is there a spending rule in place?
• How much of the organization's budget depends upon the endowment?
• Any additional institutional constraints?

Source: The William and Flora Hewlett Foundation.

not impacts the level of risk and payout of the investment portfolio. It is helpful if the board incorporates a spending rule within the IPS so that the CIO can construct an investment portfolio that takes into consideration future cash-flow needs. The spending rule is a commitment by the board that, in any given year, the cash flow needs from the investment portfolio will be limited to the agreed-upon level.

The discipline on spending budget sits with the board, not the CIO. Board members are tasked with deciding whether to maximize spending today or maximizing the probability that the organization will be able to fund payout in perpetuity. The CIO's role is to make the board aware of the implications of spending annually in excess of the return of the endowment, and then to respect the board's decision.

Another point to consider is whether the organization has additional sources of capital. In practice, rapid changes in the denominator (net asset value) create challenges for the active management of the endowment. The board should be aware of these challenges and provide as much guidance as possible, knowing that the denominator is unpredictable. University endowments and hospitals, as well as pension funds, sovereign-wealth funds, and family offices typically receive additional sources of funding into the endowment portfolio. Boards and ICs should recognize that the CIO cannot control either the contributions or the payout from the portfolio yet is responsible for maintaining the agreed-upon asset allocation policy. In light of this, there are likely to be periods when the deployment of the portfolio varies materially from the approved policy asset allocation mix.

The illiquidity tolerance of an organization needs to incorporate whether the institution's budget is flexible. Institutions with variable payout, or where the portfolio generates only a portion of the spending budget, tend to have higher illiquidity tolerance than organizations with a fixed payout or where the portfolio generates 100% of payout.

Organizations with a significant amount of multi-year commitments in the budget also have reduced flexibility in moderating spending.

> At Hewlett, 100% of the spending budget is generated by the endowment. Because of the long-term strategic work we fund through our grantees, the board and staff place great importance on maintaining the granting budget relatively stable. While Hewlett gives general operating support and mostly one-year grants, the intent of the organization is to fund work within our strategic priorities for many years and maintain staff level. This type of giving means we have some flexibility in endowment spending. Working together, Hewlett's president, CFO, and I designed a flexible budgeting mechanism whereby 80% of the budgeted spending is allocated to the programs at the start of the year, and the remaining 20% is unallocated in case spending needs to be curtailed if there is a significant market dislocation.

Another consideration in setting the investment objective is the desire of the board to incorporate non-investment criteria in the investment program. Many institutions have historically limited non-investment guidelines to prohibitions on certain types of investments. For practical purposes, even when the IPS does not specify mission-alignment, there needs to be common-sense consideration by the investment team that the portfolio should not make investments that run counter to the issue areas the organization funds.

More recently, some boards have added a request to proactively invest in a diverse set of areas that advance interests of the institution. In cases like these, the IPS should specifically state goals for the investment program, as well as the criteria that should be used in managing this type of portfolio. Below are the specific details included in Skoll Foundation's IPS as an example of the clarity the board and IC have provided the investment team regarding the evaluation of fund managers and monitoring of the investment portfolio for impact. The CIO and team accepted the new IPS and adapted the expedition plan to achieve the objective.

> Skoll's investments in external managers must be evaluated on the integration of environmental, social, and governance factors into investment strategy and process, including engagement on advancing diversity, equity, and inclusion within the investment firm. Special consideration is given to reducing net GHG [greenhouse gas] emissions attributable to the Skoll Foundation's portfolio to zero, integrating significant sustainability considerations into the investment process, and increasing mission-aligned investments that further the philanthropic objectives of the foundation. The objective is generating accretive risk-adjusted return.

Various Approaches to Policy Portfolios

While many organizations have adopted the endowment model to manage the assets of the institution, it is good practice to have a conversation with the IC to understand the benefits and drawbacks of one model versus another. It may sound like a waste of time, but a successful CIO and board should consider alternative methods for reaching the summit.

There are different approaches and strategies for an expedition. There should be a conversation about the merits and drawbacks of different models, including liquid alternatives such as the passive 70/30 equity/bond model, the high-income model, and the risk parity model, against the backdrop of the diversified asset class mix (aka endowment model). There are also a number of models that combine a mix of direct investments in equity of companies or property, with third-party-managed public and private funds.

Every asset allocation approach has different risk/reward scenarios and the implications on the probability that an institution is able to achieve the investment objective set forth by the board. Below are brief overviews of other models used:

- The traditional 70% equity/30% fixed income portfolio: This model can be invested on a passive basis and rebalanced monthly. The advantages of this approach are that it is simple to understand, implement, and monitor, is fully liquid, and is low cost. Unfortunately, it is expected to generate low returns relative to other approaches with higher volatility and drawdowns.

- The high-income portfolio: This approach is based on the theory that the primary objective of the portfolio is to generate annual cash flow to meet liabilities (grants and expenses). There is no obvious index to reference here, so a mix of investment-grade and high-yield indices can be combined and easily constructed. Unfortunately, while this portfolio reduces the variability around funding a set level of spending, the probability of a large drawdown remains high (as occurred in 2022), and the probability of maintaining the real (inflation-adjusted) spending power of the endowment is low relative to other approaches.

- The risk parity portfolio: The risk parity portfolio tries to diversify exposure to various sources of portfolio risk, rather than taking a concentrated exposure to equity risk premium as occurs in most traditional portfolios. There are many ways investors choose to implement a risk parity framework, yet at its core is the belief that one should allocate capital based on risk factors instead of asset classes by using

Sharpe Ratios. Risk premia are calculated on a backward-looking basis and assume that the relationships between asset classes and risk are relatively unchanged in the future. On a backward-looking basis, risk parity portfolios have demonstrated success in generating superior returns and lower volatility than alternate approaches, primarily due to the benefit of strong returns in levered bonds (2010–2020). However, normalizing expected bond returns into this approach, the expected return and risk profile of the portfolio is sub-optimal. The risk parity framework, by its very nature, requires 2–3× gross exposure (leverage) and a large allocation to bonds, both impractical for a typical institution.

Figure 1.1 shows the expected return per unit of risk of the various approaches. The endowment model has the highest expected annualized return, but it also has the highest expected volatility. An institution that prefers less volatility could be best served by portfolio approaches with more fixed income exposure like the high-income or risk parity models. There is no one perfect model for all portfolios or institutions. In guiding the conversation with the IC and board, the CIO can ask:

- How will the IC and the board feel if public equity and bond market returns exceed the diversified mix for one or two years?
- How will the IC and the board feel if peer institutions are reporting higher returns because peers have a higher level of illiquid assets?
- If the IC wants to have direct equity exposure, is it prepared for significantly greater volatility of returns?

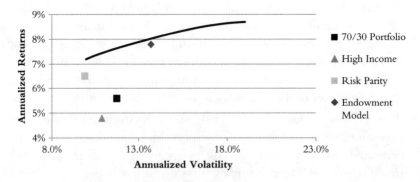

Figure 1.1 Estimated Risk vs. Reward by Portfolio Types
Source: The William and Flora Hewlett Foundation, July 2019.

By openly discussing alternative models, the IC can agree to the approach that is right for their organization and hire an expedition leader (the CIO) that has the skill set to reach the objective. Depending on the specific objectives of the organization, the endowment model with illiquid assets may not be a suitable approach. Better to know that before it is too late!

Risk Tolerance

The balance between risk and return requires thinking about two different paths. The CIO could construct a conservative portfolio to minimize short-term volatility and drawdown risk. This would reduce the near-term threat of a decline in the value of the portfolio in any given year, but only by also reducing the expected return of the portfolio below the typical level of payout, thereby diminishing spending power over time. Market volatility can at times be good because it provides an opportunity to take advantage of opportunities and capture upside. As a matter of practice, then, institutions choose to accept short-term volatility in order to minimize the long-term risk of declining real value. An institution that does not take sufficient risk in the investment program is likely to under-earn payout over time, and erode the value of the endowment, making it difficult to imagine that the institution can be funded in perpetuity.

Assessing the true risk tolerance of a board typically made up of well-intentioned individuals is difficult. Individually, they may know their risk tolerance; however, as a board member it is challenging to understand the risk tolerance of the institution. In practice, there are a variety of conversations between the board, the president, and the CIO that should occur at the start of an investment program and then continue to be had every few years.

Defining risk naturally follows from the conversations between the CIO and the board. At the board level, it is helpful to understand what one or two items would cause anxiety for the board and the institution. A successful CIO listens to each member of the board and weaves these concerns into a series of questions. For many boards, the two primary areas of anxiety related to the investment portfolio are: (1) the long-term viability of the institution and the financial support the organization requires from the portfolio, and (2) the impact on retaining and recruiting talented staff to deliver the mission of the organization. Table 1.3 provides

Table 1.3

Conversation Starters with IC and Board
• Does the institution have a perpetual or spend-down model?
• Does the institution have a spending rule?
• What level of risk is appropriate for your specific institution?
• Does the board fully understand the potential drawdown of the portfolio?
• Does the board agree on investing with a long-term horizon, and are incentives aligned with the vision?
• Does the board agree on the objective but in meetings focus on returns relative to peers?
• How will the board react if public equity and bond returns are higher than the multi-asset class portfolio for one or two years?
• Will the board be patient and stand firm in support of the investment program during challenging times?

Source: The William and Flora Hewlett Foundation.

a list of things to consider in conversations with the board and IC. Refreshing the conversation regarding the level of risk should take place every three to five years.

One of the ways to arrive at risk tolerance is to determine the willingness of the institution to change the level of spending. Being direct and asking how the board would respond if the mark-to-market value of the portfolio declined by 20% is likely a good place to start the conversation. Another way to arrive at the issue is to assess whether there is an expectation that "eating" (funding spending by reducing the corpus instead of by generating investment returns) into the endowment is the natural course of action during a downturn, or if the expectation is that the board will reduce spending to mitigate the reduction in the long-term real value of the portfolio. The CIO needs to be sensitive to the fact the board is responsible for balancing the priority of maintaining the long-term mission of the organization and staffing level, against the desire to take increased risk in the investment portfolio.

It also helps the conversation to consider what the organization would be able to do if the value of the endowment increased by 20%. Admittedly, it may sound odd that a conversation about a successful investment program should also be part of determining the IPS, but it is critically important for one reason alone: if the institution would be unable to absorb a larger endowment due to the narrow mission or simply because it would be unable to staff in a responsible manner, then the CIO and board need to take this into consideration in developing the IPS.

Additionally, the CIO and the IC should determine whether the institution has a tolerance for using leverage at the portfolio level. Does the portfolio have enough flexibility to add levered beta? Typically, endowments that use leverage tend to use modest amounts (up to 15%) and have a secure line of credit in place (usually one year's worth of spending) to manage cash flows in the event of a drawdown in the investment portfolio.

The conversation regarding risk tolerance of the board and the IC could be framed using considerations listed in Table 1.4.

Refreshing the conversation every few years regarding the level of risk the institution is willing to tolerate also helps to clarify for the board the potential downside of the investment program. Some institutions review the policy portfolio and risk annually, while some have more frequent conversations with the IC, but review with the full board every three years. It has been my experience that a forewarned board is prepared and patient for the eventual recovery, whereas a board that has not had a recent conversation about risk tends to question the investment program at the most inopportune times.

> In March of 2008, we thought it would be a good idea (with no idea how useful it would turn out to be) to update the full board on several key elements of the Hewlett portfolio. We reviewed the policy portfolio asset allocation mix and discussed the level of risk we were taking to have a high probability of achieving the return objective. Importantly, we explained the potential for the portfolio to suffer a 20% decline in value over a period of ten years. We prepared the board members for the eventuality that at some point during their tenure as board members they would sit in the boardroom and listen to me report a significant decline in the value of the endowment. Markets were healthy in March of 2008, so they listened but likely thought it was a theoretical exercise.

Table 1.4

Risk Tolerance Framework
• Clear objective (maximize return, preserve real spending power in perpetuity, mission-alignment, etc.)
• Amount institution needs annually to draw from the endowment
• Flexibility in level of spending
• Use of leverage
• Output from stress tests

Source: The William and Flora Hewlett Foundation.

When I reported at the November 2008 board meeting the value of the endowment had declined 20%, the board was not surprised and simply asked how we were adapting the investment plan to ensure the program could weather the storm and position the portfolio for opportunities ahead. Some of my peers were not as fortunate, and the surprise of their boards and IC at the decline in value of their endowments resulted in a strong recommendation or mandate to reduce risk and make inopportune changes to the investment program.

Time Horizon

Beyond agreement on objectives and risk tolerance, there needs to be agreement on the time horizon the board and the institution will use to judge the success of the investment program. Some boards and CIOs may take as a given that the organization has a long-term horizon. Experience has taught me that in practice, individual board members and institutions may have divergent views on the time it takes a CIO to deliver on the agreed-upon objectives.

While successful investment programs are focused on generating superior investment returns over long horizons of 10–20 years, a CIO must constantly balance between short-term (three-year goals) and long-term goals. Having an agreed-upon time horizon, whether short-term or long-term, will help avoid surprises on either side and ensure continuity of the strategic direction of the program. There are several reasons why it is wise to agree on the time horizon of the investment program.

First, the time frame upon which the investment strategy and the investment team will be judged is likely to impact asset allocation. Consider the type of asset mix a CIO would propose if the board expected to judge success of a program in 1 year, or 5 years, versus an agreement that success would be judged 10–15 years out.

Second, as the members of the IC and board change over time, the CIO needs to ensure that all new fiduciaries are aware of the agreed-upon time horizon of the program in order to keep the strategy on course, especially if there are illiquid strategies in the asset mix. The greater the allocation to illiquid strategies, the more important it is that there be full alignment in expectations between the CIO and the board since, by definition, the strategic direction of a portfolio cannot be easily altered.

Lastly, communicating the institution's investment strategy and time horizon is essential in securing allocations in sought-after investment managers and in recruiting and retaining investment team staff. Investment managers want long-term partners that can be counted on as a reliable source of capital. Similarly, the investment team relies on the mentorship and leadership of the CIO to do their jobs well, and to advance their careers. Transparency in time horizon eliminates confusion among all stakeholders.

Unfortunately, not all institutions have boards or ICs that understand the importance of good governance. There are institutions that seem to always look at the upside in terms of the long-term secular story, but the communication with the CIO is based on the short-term cyclical opportunity and return profile. Whenever CIOs at these institutions report progress on the investment strategy, the IC's investment horizon contracts because the short-term risks seem to cloud the summit.

Of course, there are occasions when an institution decides on an entirely different direction that is no longer served by the existing investment program. This should not reflect poorly on the CIO or the board; it simply is a new reality that must be dealt with. Typically, this occurs when pools of assets are merged into a single-pool vehicle (e.g., hospital systems or different schools within a university), or a foundation receives a transformational donation. When a transformative event occurs, a new IPS should be developed, and a new strategic portfolio designed to achieve the new objective of the organization.

I leave you with one last example of how expedition leaders need to adapt. During the 2008 crisis, the Hewlett investment program was able to adapt, reassess the objective, identify resources and skills needed to overcome the immediate hazard, and improve the resilience of the portfolio, with the full support of the IC and board. It was a time when anxiety at the organization was high, yet the confidence in the investment team and constant communication allowed the investment program the room to improve.

The diversified portfolio we had carefully constructed suffered a serious drawdown in value between October 2008 and March 2009 during the Great Financial Crisis (GFC). Asset classes that we believed would provide diversification benefit failed to do so. Unanticipated liquidity gaps in parts of the capital markets made transacting difficult. The portfolio had sufficient liquidity to fund grants and capital calls, but was not in a position to lean in to take advantage of attractive opportunities.

We adapted the expedition plan to prevent the situation from happening in the future. We created more robust risk and cash flow models. We secured two lines of credit to fund one year of payout from different banks; one secured line and an unsecured line. We also changed the way we thought about spending and created flexibility in the annual budget. Finally, we amended the IPS to adjust the annual payout down more quickly to protect the long-term value of the endowment.

The clarity of communication throughout the prior years leading up to the GFC, and soundness of the plan to steer the endowment forward, allowed us to manage the anxiety that naturally exists during these moments in both investment team and IC. The board and the IC showed confidence and support; both were critical to allowing the team to adapt the plan and continue the trek to the summit.

2

Defining Governance Responsibilities

The silent clash of ideals . . . had taught me something; that the challenge to us was not only the mountains we planned to climb but the way we would come to terms with one another's very different views on climbing and living.

—Greg Child[1]

Achieving the investment objective of the institution is truly a team sport. Once there is agreement by the board on the investment objective and risk tolerance, the board must determine the extent to which it is comfortable delegating authority of fiduciary oversight and management of the investment program.

Governance responsibilities must be determined to ensure accountability and provide the investment team with the freedom to do their job. While the primary responsibility for setting and implementing the investment strategy is entirely that of the CIO, the board and the president of the institution also serve as key supports during the life of the investment program. In my experience, clear delegation of authority and transparency in communication between the CIO and the board are essential for the health of the institution, the investment program, and the staff.

---

[1] Greg Child, *Thin Air: Encounters in the Himalayas* (Mountaineers Books, 1998).

In practice, the CIO has often been hired before the very important conversations about the investment objective and delegation take place. Being a CIO or expedition leader takes a great deal of commitment. The CIO is faced with lots of small and large decisions every day. The board needs to consider whether the CIO enjoys complexity and solving problems. More importantly, the board needs to have confidence the CIO has the strength of character to lead when things get hard, shares the values of the organization, and is known for helping investment teams thrive.

Delegation comes with responsibility to do two things: manage the investment portfolio and manage the team. Much of this book is dedicated to techniques that can be used to successfully manage an investment portfolio. That said, the CIO must also assemble a team with the stamina and drive to make it to the summit, as well as being dedicated to the mission of the organization. The attributes of building and managing a high-performing investment team are covered in detail in Chapter 13. The ability to thrive through good times and work through the difficult ones is greatly helped by a commitment to transparent and frequent communication.

Delegation of Authority

The board typically delegates the review and oversight of the investment portfolio to a subset of the board called the investment committee (IC). The IC has the fiduciary responsibility for oversight of the investment assets. It is charged with ensuring the assets are invested in a prudent manner. The IC is authorized, via a board resolution, to review and recommend changes to the Investment Policy Statement (IPS) for full approval by the board. The resolution authorizes the IC to make all decisions related to implementation of the investment program.

The IC may be advised by outside consultants in the initial decision whether to hire an internal CIO and investment team, or that the institution could be served by an outsourced investment management solution. Most often the outsourced solution is an investment management firm that specializes in managing multi-asset class portfolios. The IC typically weighs the cost and ability to recruit and retain an internal investment team against the benefits offered by outsourced solutions.

Institutions with under $1 billion in assets typically have ICs that are less familiar with investment programs. These institutions may engage a consultant to recommend either a fully passive, public market allocation managed by a low-cost index fund provider, or an outsourced CIO solution where the investment assets are pooled alongside other small institutions to form a diversified pool of strategies. While the IC may entirely delegate the implementation of the investment strategy, the IC remains accountable to the board for achieving the investment objective.

Institutions with endowment pools above $1 billion are usually able to recruit board members and IC members with familiarity with investment programs. In the past 20 years, a majority of institutions of this size have created an in-house investment office. Achieving the investment objective is the shared responsibility of the IC and the CIO. The board resolution authorizes the CIO to act on behalf of the organization in matters related to the investment program.

Extent of Delegation

There is no right level of delegation. The extent to which responsibility is delegated depends on the culture of the institution and the degree of trust that has been built between the CIO and the IC. As the IC develops trust with the CIO and the team, the delegation of authority can and should be revisited.

As with every relationship, trust is built over time, and the IC chair and CIO together can decide when the moment is right to cede greater responsibility to the CIO. The importance of the role of the IC chair should not be underestimated. Scott Malpass, the legendary CIO of the University of Notre Dame, benefited from the stability of having only two IC chairs during his 32-year tenure at the institution. The essential consideration is that each institution is unique in their stage of development and should delegate authority only to the degree to which they are comfortable. It is wise to avoid pushing delegation beyond the comfort of the IC simply because when things go wrong, the IC needs to fully trust the CIO.

Whatever the extent of delegation is for a particular institution, there needs to be consistent and frequent communication between the CIO and IC chair on a variety of topics that may arise but don't fall neatly into the agreed-upon delegation grid. The IC chair serves as a sounding board for the CIO, and together they determine whether a topic is material enough to be brought up to the entire IC or whether the issue is immaterial and can be reported at the following meeting. The IC chair should also inform the CIO of any issues arising at the board that could impact the investment program. Consistency in the IC chair provides stability to the investment program and team. Most successful investment programs have benefited greatly from having an IC chair serve in the role for a decade or more.

Newly established investment programs may require time to develop trust and delegation of responsibility to the investment team. It takes time for IC members to trust that the investment strategy is sound and that the proper due diligence is being undertaken on every investment. That said, in the past several years, several highly experienced peers have moved from established investment programs to new organizations where they have been able to adopt the same delegation of authority they worked under at their prior institution since the IC is familiar with their skills.

The more established investment programs have many years of proven experience in creating investment strategies, managing risk, and earning the trust of their ICs. A trusting relationship between the CIO and the IC allows the CIO to lean in when markets dislocate and new attractive investment opportunities suddenly surface. It also provides the freedom to develop new frameworks and implement strategies before they become evident to the market. At its most optimal level, full delegation of authority frees up the CIO and the team's time to focus on managing the portfolio.

Breaking down potential delegation into five areas may allow the conversation between the CIO and the IC to focus on areas of agreement and established trust. The objective is to establish either joint or sole responsibility for various parts of the investment program. Many IC and board members find it challenging to understand the level of detail and engagement at which they should be asking questions. The best board members have years of experience and know exactly the level at which to think strategically, without being pulled into the weeds. As the title of the section implies, the IC has the choice to delegate or retain responsibility. Table 2.1 lists a handful of areas to start the conversation.

A simple three-level delegation matrix tends to clarify where responsibility and accountability lie and serves as a reference document for legal documentation requiring delegation of authority to the CIO. For each of the areas of responsibility that can be delegated to the CIO, noted in Table 2.1, the CIO and the IC should agree on the type of delegation. The levels of delegation are noted in Table 2.2.

Some ICs may want to limit their decision-making responsibilities to approving the asset allocation policy, rebalancing ranges, and portfolio risk level proposed by the CIO. In doing so, the IC co-owns the exposure

Table 2.1

Areas of Responsibility
• Asset allocation policy and risk tolerance
• Rebalancing ranges
• Benchmark selection
• Hiring of managers
• Hiring of custodian and consultants

Source: The William and Flora Hewlett Foundation.

Table 2.2

Levels of Delegation
• Must be formally approved by the IC
• Notification via email without need for approval
• Notification in writing at the following meeting

Source: The William and Flora Hewlett Foundation.

to capital markets (beta) of the portfolio alongside the CIO, and delegates to the CIO the implementation of the policy portfolio and generation of alpha. This includes hiring and firing of managers, custodians, and consultants.

Nearly all ICs choose to retain the responsibility of approving the benchmark or benchmarks they will use to judge the success of the investment program. Retention of benchmark selection is considered best practice, since it establishes an independent and objective process for evaluating the success of the investment team. By separating the duties of oversight and evaluation from the CIO's role in managing the portfolio, the compensation committee of the board is able to objectively incentivize and retain the investment team.

There is no best practice in terms of delegation related to hiring of managers. Some ICs consider their primary role as an advisor to the team in selecting investment-manager firms. The composition of the IC may be made up of experienced investors that can offer access to highly sought-after funds and off-reference-list insights that could be useful to the team. They may want to be involved in every decision to hire or fire an individual manager. Other ICs are members of the board with limited investing experience and benefit from having a great deal of trust in the due diligence process and investment strategy implementation. These ICs delegate discretion to the CIO for all but very large investments (typically defined as 2% of the portfolio).

In order to maximize the time that the CIO and the investment team spend on investment-related matters and to improve the probability of a successful climb to the summit, the institution needs to consider not only the freedom of delegation, but also what tools and team are required for a successful ascent. A broad delegation of authority provides the team with "lightweight gear" that empowers them to face long routes, navigate icy patches, and endure unforeseen changes in weather conditions. Flexibility in the moment is a competitive edge in managing the endowment.

The evolution of delegation of authority at Hewlett is useful in showing how delegation adapts as the investment program develops and matures. The Hewlett board delegated authority over the investment program to the IC over three decades ago. For the first decade, the IC had complete responsibility for the investment program. In 2004, as the Hewlett investment program finished selling the stock of HP and Agilent left by William Hewlett upon his death, and developed the current investment program, the board and then CIO, Laurie Hoagland, created a new delegation of authority.

Hewlett's delegation of authority is deeply rooted in the culture of the organization. The Hewlett family believes in hiring high-quality people and letting them have the freedom to excel. This is a core principle of the Hewlett Foundation. Therefore, it was very much in line with this philosophy that the delegation of authority was very broad-based for the time. It helped tremendously that Laurie Hoagland was trusted by the board, having served as the first CIO for Stanford University's endowment, and as the IC chair prior to joining Hewlett as its first CIO in 2002. At the time, the Hewlett IC decided to retain the responsibility for approving asset allocation policy, rebalancing ranges, and the benchmark. The hiring of new managers required a notification in writing to the IC (but not approval). Any termination of manager or decision to not commit to a new fund raised by an existing private manager was communicated in the IC materials at the subsequent meeting.

A decade ago, the Hewlett IC agreed to make a small change to the delegation of authority related to the hiring of managers. In part, the review of the delegation of authority arose naturally as the Hewlett portfolio reached maturity and much of the activity of the team was focused on re-underwriting existing managers in the portfolio. The IC communicated a desire to remain focused on capital allocation, risk, and performance relative to benchmarks. While they appreciated being informed of new managers we planned to hire, they recognized their greatest value was in the strategic direction of the investment program. The process was streamlined so that nearly all actions taken by the CIO are communicated to the IC at the subsequent meeting, allowing the team to focus its energy on managing the portfolio.

Governance

Clearly setting out the responsibilities of the trustees and the advisors to the IC proves helpful in setting expectations of the role they are expected to serve. By creating a simple one- or two-page document, the organization is able to define the "job description" of an IC member or advisor so they understand their role in ensuring that the endowment is appropriately managed. This document should state the responsibilities defined in the Delegation of Authority. It should also state the years of a term of service and renewal of membership to the IC.

There is no single correct way to think about the composition of the IC. Some organizations choose to have a handful of trustees or board members serve on the IC even though most board members are not investment professionals. Other organizations, typically family offices or sovereign wealth funds, tend to have ICs consisting of many members but the power resides with one or two key decision makers. The practical advice is simply that the less experience the board members have with investments, the greater the benefit to the investment program of attracting multiple external advisors with investment experience.

Criteria for selecting external advisors to the IC should be clearly stated. Their primary role is to serve as advisors to the IC in investment matters that may require deeper industry knowledge than may be possessed by the board members constituting the IC. Ideally, IC advisors have investment experience through various market cycles. IC advisors should, as a group, have investing skills in various asset classes. Some organizations form subcommittees of the board for each major asset class and invite external advisors to advise the team and IC. The highly talented CIO of Williams College, Collette Chilton, has found asset class subcommittees to be helpful to the investment team and program. It is important the IC advisors have the time to engage in discussions with the CIO and investment team and be eager to share their wisdom gained over decades of investing in their organizations. Advisors should also understand the mission of the organization and agree with the investment objective set in the IPS.

Assembling the Team

Once the objectives and delegation of authority have been agreed upon, the CIO needs to make an honest assessment of the skill level and role of every member of the team. Frequently, CIOs assume responsibility for existing investment teams and are left with the decision of whether to keep the team that is in place or hire a team with different skills and experience. In Chapter 13, we delve deeper into recruiting and managing a team during the expedition. As the investment program prepares for base camp, the IC and CIO must identify the skill sets needed, the number of staff required to achieve the objective, and the tools and infrastructure required for a successful climb.

Every CIO has a certain set of preferences, skills, and management style that they believe will improve the probability of success. It is not uncommon for an institution to experience significant turnover in the investment team when a new CIO is hired. This happens most often when the CIO has been hired to change the way the investment program is managed since new skill sets are needed to implement the new strategy.

The board should be supportive of changes to the investment team as a new CIO assumes the role simply because the skill sets needed for a successful climb with a new CIO are likely different from what was needed with prior leadership. Despite the discomfort this may cause the organization, this is a difficult decision that in hindsight is rarely regretted. The CIO needs to trust that the team has the skills, resiliency, and work ethic to make it to the summit. Likewise, the investment team must trust the CIO to lead them successfully and be willing to shift strategy at any moment.

It is important for the CIO to be careful and take time in assembling the team. A strong climbing team has the skill set to climb, but also has experience using different approaches and tools from those of the CIO and each other. Intellectually curious people who are willing to accept constructive feedback are great team members. A CIO is well served by observing the behavior of the members of the team and each person's ability to think clearly, form strategies, and adapt to the changes in the environment.

Many of the most successful CIOs select a strong number two that complements their skill set. One of the most famous duos was David Swensen and Dean Takahashi, who worked together from 1986 to 2019 to lead Yale's endowment into alternative assets and generate consistently superior returns. Typically, a number two is someone who isn't afraid to challenge the CIO and who is able to come up with different ways of moving forward from the CIO. Importantly, a well-chosen number two is someone with the strength of character to continue moving forward even when they disagree with the CIO's decision. Naturally, this type of trust can only be built over time after facing several daunting challenges, and after the CIO willingly admits her approach may be, at times, wrong and she is willing to consider other options.

It is difficult to identify who will surface as the number two as the climbing team is formed. However, during the ascent from base camp to first and second camp, the CIO has the opportunity to observe the strengths and failings of every member of the team. By the time the team is facing the challenges of portfolio construction and active management (moving from first camp through to third camp), the person identified as number two usually becomes obvious to the CIO and to the rest of the team. This is especially evident during challenging moments, as the values and priorities of the CIO and the number two are often the same.

At Hewlett, I have had the fortune of having an excellent number two, Brett Johnson. Brett and I have worked together for over a decade. At the beginning, it was not clear he would become such a critical member of the expedition. Over a number of years, watching his ability to think clearly in the face of adversity and his eagerness to refine every part of our process, it became obvious I needed to learn more from him. My style is intuitive and strategic. His is linear and analytical. We support each other in every moment when we have to stop, evaluate, and reconsider the best plan forward. Critically, there is never a doubt in my mind that we both have the same goal – to make it to the summit.

Brett and I raise the bar for each other and are determined to generate consistently superior returns for the Hewlett endowment. We have each other's back to ensure the team makes it to the summit. Climbers refer to this connection as the "brotherhood of the rope."[2] Of course, there are times when we disagree on the best approach forward or a way to avoid making a mistake. Brett challenges me to keep pushing limits and aim higher. Given Brett's experience climbing with me for more than a decade, he could lead his own expedition. However, we know that the probability of success in reaching the summit of this mountain, and every subsequent peak, is better because we climb together.

---

[2] The term "brotherhood of the rope" refers to the interdependence among members of a climbing team for survival and success. It is also the title of a biography of a famous American doctor attempting a climb on K2 in 1953.

Some CIOs resist developing a number two because they may believe they are more than capable of making all the decisions and setting the course for the investment program. Some may not want to be vulnerable to experiencing the loss of a trusted climbing partner and prefer to have a distance between the CIO and the rest of the team. Others may simply not want the challenge of having another strong investor on the team. After all, having another strong investor with good ideas on how to navigate markets could feel like a threat. The team probably wouldn't appreciate having strategic plans altered by dissenting opinions. These concerns are real; however, the most successful investors have had the benefit of a trusted sounding board. The benefits to the team and the institution far outweigh the concerns.

The benefits to the success of the expedition and the CIO of having a number two are numerous. Being a CIO is a lonely job filled with difficult and frequent decisions. It is an exhausting job if done correctly. There are many people depending on the success of the CIO and the expedition team. There is more than enough worry and burden to share with a trusted partner. In addition, events outside the investment office can temporarily reduce the CIO's focus on the portfolio. CIOs are not machines. CIOs want to excel at their job as well as retain a personal life that nourishes their soul. At some point, every CIO who has had the incredible luck of having a trusted number two has had the ability to catch their breath, simply because the number two was able to step up and lead the team forward for a brief period of time.

On a practical level, solving problems and finding solutions to tough challenges is best done by two people who can test each other and talk through the potential pitfalls of the strategy without egos getting in the way. Having another person with whom the CIO can be honest about the risks of the strategy is likely to produce better decisions.

There are numerous examples when two heads (Brett and mine) were much better than one, but I will note one example to provide an idea of how integrative thinking can deliver a better decision than if either one of us would have approached the situation on our own. Integrative thinking refers to the practice of building on each other's last idea and improving it or finding the counterpoint and solving it. I have learned that when the two of us independently want to discuss an idea, it is worth sitting in front of a whiteboard to understand it from every aspect.

A few years ago, Brett and I were whiteboarding the strategy of the part of the portfolio that serves as ballast to counterbalance equity risk. He had assessed the go-forward expected return of each manager and the position size in the endowment. My question was the efficiency of the various managers in terms of probability of delivering expected return relative to the risk contribution to the portfolio. Several of the managers had expected return within a narrow band, which meant this lens was not going to provide much insight into sizing the various manager exposures. The question then became the confidence we each had in each manager's ability to execute their strategy and generate consistent alpha. The decision became clear as we discussed the implementation of the strategy. Within a few hours, working together we were able to develop a new framework that has materially improved the return profile of the portfolio.

Unfortunately, sometimes there is a realization that despite best efforts, the team is not quite functioning at the highest level. Humility is helpful at these moments. When assembling the team, the CIO never really knows if a member of the team has the stamina, discipline, and work ethic to make it to the top. If a CIO finds there is someone on the team who no longer has the drive to push themselves or is exhibiting signs of burnout and is holding the team back, it is best to make the difficult decision and leave them behind at the next camp.

There are more frequent rescue missions from various points on any mountain climb than are reported. None of these decisions to turn back and join another team are tragic; they simply reflect the humanity involved in intense sports like alpinism and investing. In nearly every case, the team will be relieved, and the person will have the freedom to find another team for the descent and to attempt to climb a different mountain.

Investment team compensation sometimes is difficult for organizations to understand. In Chapter 13, we spend time on managing the investment team and designing incentive programs. Typically, the market sets compensation for the investment team, not the individual institution. On a practical basis, the first step is for the CIO to work with the IC chair and compensation committee to establish a philosophy on pay. Then the CIO and HR can evaluate the market data and use it as a guide, taking into account differences in experience, responsibilities, and so on. The value created by the investment team should more than compensate for the cost of the investment office.

One of the ways an institution can gain comfort in the investment team's compensation structure is to ensure there is a formalized and rigorous review of each member's contribution to the objective. For example, Hewlett has a detailed review process that helps to highlight for the compensation committee the strengths and contributions of every team member, that also notes the specific areas for improvement for the following year. Additionally we have an agreed-upon compensation philosophy using market data collected by our compensation consultant. We create ranges within each investment professional level based on years of experience and contribution to the portfolio. Ideally, given our open-door approach and culture of continuous feedback and learning, no one on the investment team should be surprised about their total compensation.

Transparency into the Investment Process

Implicitly, by delegating authority, the board and IC trust the CIO to set and implement the strategic direction of the investment program, develop the infrastructure to support the work, and keep improving the investment process. As we previously noted, it takes time to develop trust. While trust is being developed, the IC and the CIO need to consider intentionality and the fact that the CIO and IC are aligned in creating good outcomes. Successful CIOs ask the IC for advice to enhance collaboration.

As CIO, I provide the IC with a strategic vision of the investment program that lays out the strategy for generating the expected return, at the agreed-upon level of risk, over the coming decade. Every asset class team provides an in-depth portfolio construction and manager review once a year to the IC, where manager decisions are discussed.

A predictable and rigorous process provides confidence during the period when trust is being developed. Specifically, one of the easiest ways to develop trust is for the CIO to offer the IC members the opportunity to delve deep into any decision of an individual investment manager to gain familiarity with the robust due diligence and oversight process conducted by the investment team. Likewise, the IC can proactively work to build trust by spending time understanding the strategic tilts in asset class strategies and the overall portfolio. When the IC believes the CIO is adhering to strong processes, they are more likely to encourage investing against prevailing consensus and being patient during difficult times.

Broad delegation of authority also comes with the commitment by the CIO to full transparency and accountability. The CIO commits to frequent and transparent communication, so the IC is able to effectively do its fiduciary job of ensuring the portfolio is being managed in accordance with the agreed-upon policy. In practice, the CIO shares both good and challenging news, and listens to the concerns of the IC in formulating a plan of action.

One of the proudest moments as a CIO occurred when I realized that the incredible trust the Hewlett IC has in my ability as an investor and leader extended to the entire expedition team. A few years ago, one of my great climbing partners, Christy Richardson, realized she was ready to climb an entirely different type of mountain. The loss of any member of the expedition is challenging, but losing Christy was hard on a personal level. She was part of my *brotherhood of the rope* and I lost someone that I knew would always have my back and prevent the portfolio from suffering great loss. That said, she did me and the institution a great service in mentoring her number two for five years before she left. She taught him her extraordinary high bar for manager selection and portfolio management, and how to work collaboratively with the team. When I called the IC chair to deliver the news of Christy's amazing new adventure, he immediately agreed with my suggestion to promote her number two to take over as director of several private asset classes. After consulting further with the president and advisors, it was clear that their trust and confidence in our process and our alignment reached well beyond me and the asset class directors. They were sure that her number two had received the training in both technical and soft skills to succeed as our new asset class head. It was one of those moments when the time invested in governance and communication really paid off.

Settling in at Base Camp

3

The Subtlety
of Public Markets

Think with me here . . . everyone wants to be on the mountaintop, but if you'll remember, mountaintops are rocky and cold. There is no growth on the top of a mountain. Sure, the view is great, but what's a view for? A view just gives us a glimpse of our next destination – our next target. But to hit that target, we must come off the mountain, go through the valley, and begin to climb the next slope. It is in the valley that we slog through the lush grass and rich soil, learning and becoming what enables us to summit life's next peak.

—Andy Andrews[1]

You may think it is a waste of time slogging through the valley to consider the intended role of each public asset class because asset class headings seem so obvious. I caution against this because I am always surprised when I ask 10 investors what the role is of public equity, or hedge funds, or fixed income in their portfolio, I usually hear at least five or more different answers. Instead, consider the process of clarifying the role of the asset class and the most efficient way to deliver the highest risk-adjusted return as a great problem to solve.

---

[1]Andy Andrews, *The Noticer: Sometimes, All a Person Needs Is a Little Perspective* (Thomas Nelson, 2011).

Public assets give investors an incredible number of tools to implement numerous strategies and, in most cases, provide liquidity and flexibility to the portfolio. They can serve as an effective tool to manage underlying exposure in the portfolio to economic factors, interest rates, and growth.

At the highest level, the role of public assets in a diversified portfolio is to provide exposure to the return generated by public markets (beta), provide flexibility in managing exposure to markets, and serve as a source of funding to meet spending obligations. On a practical level, it is often helpful to have a view of what you want each of the public asset classes to contribute to the overall portfolio before you start building the policy portfolio. Table 3.1 has a few questions to think about in terms of how public asset classes fit into the needs of the investment program.

The Role of Public Assets

Public markets have an investable index to provide exposure to the investment opportunity. Investors are able to buy the market (beta) exposure using passive bond and equity investment vehicles, hiring active bond and equity fund managers, or buying public equities and bonds directly for the institution, to be managed by an in-house team. Both in terms of measuring alpha (return in excess of the benchmark) and understanding intended and unintended sector or geographic tilts, investors have a readily available bond or equity index against which to compare. Every institution has different needs for liquidity and differentiated

Table 3.1

Questions to Consider Before Developing a Policy Portfolio
• What is the role we want the asset class to have, in this portfolio and for this institution, to achieve the goal of this organization?
• Does the institution's investment team have the access to top-tier managers and to the necessary experience to underwrite active public managers?
• Will investing be done only through external managers, or will there be some in-house management?
• Should passive exposure be part of the strategy within an asset class?
• How will active-manager and hedge fund lock-up structures impact portfolio flexibility?
• Over what time frame will performance be measured?

Source: The William and Flora Hewlett Foundation.

access to managers that have the potential to consistently outperform the benchmark. Table 3.2 lists the four primary considerations in constructing a public equity and/or bond portfolio.

Table 3.2

Considerations for Public Assets
1. Passive versus active
2. External managers versus in-house management
3. Regional/sector exposure
4. Factor-based/market capitalization exposure

Source: The William and Flora Hewlett Foundation.

Capturing Growth in Public Equities

The role of public equity is to generate returns from growth in companies through capital appreciation, dividends, and stock buybacks. There are two primary sources of risk in public equities: volatility/drawdown, and idiosyncratic company risk. The theoretical return available from investing in public equities is captured in the equity risk premium (ERP). ERP is the expected premium an investor demands to be paid over the risk-free rate (typically the yield on U.S. three-month Treasury bill) to take equity risk. The equity risk premium cannot be easily observed.

Exposure to equity markets is referred to as beta of 1.0. Beta refers to how an individual asset moves when the stock market rises or falls. Investors must make decisions about the source of equity market (beta) exposure they seek. The first step is to consider passive versus active management. Once that is decided, the expedition leader can consider whether and to what extent the public equity portfolio should be managed by external managers rather than an in-house equity team.

Passive equity has grown enormously over the past 20 years and now represents a majority of the trading volume in equity markets globally. There are two main types of passive instrument: exchange-traded funds (ETFs) and passive mutual funds. The main difference between the two is that investors can trade ETFs intraday but mutual funds orders get executed at the end of the trading day. In the past five years, the cost of passive equity exposure has fallen significantly. If the role in the portfolio is to generate the return from market beta, and to do so at low cost and without introducing active risk, then passive investing is an efficient way to obtain exposure.

If the role in the portfolio is to generate returns from both market beta and alpha (excess return above the index), then hiring active equity managers provides the portfolio with the opportunity to earn alpha. Active equity exposure has evolved over the past 20 years. In the 1990s, large investment management firms offered multiple active equity products that closely tracked the benchmark indices. The objective was to generate some alpha by underweighting or overweighting the top 50 names or so in an index and to do it consistently year after year. As passive exposure became easier and more cost effective to implement in institutional portfolios, it became more challenging for active managers to compete, since consistently generating 100 basis points of alpha is very hard to do and the management fee drag reduced the net return even further. Today's successful active public equity firms manage portfolios that are highly differentiated from the index to be able to generate returns, net of fees, above the index. We will consider, what, if any, additional risk CIOs need to consider in evaluating the active risk taken by active mandates in Chapter 7.

Finally, investors need to decide whether the portfolio will be managed entirely through external managers, or if some or all of the assets will be managed in house. Allocating to passive index strategies is typically done by the same team that is responsible for allocating to managers, in contrast to active in-house management of assets that requires an experienced group of professional investors whose primary responsibility is the management of the internally managed equity portfolio. Their risk-adjusted performance is judged relative to the external managers of the institution.

There are advantages and disadvantages to in-house active equity management. The advantage is that it is typically less expensive to manage in house than to pay fees to external active managers. Also, if the institution wants to own a select group of stocks for a 5- to 10-year horizon for strategic reasons, then it may make sense to avoid the fees associated with active management. The disadvantages are that external active managers may be reluctant to share information if they believe the in-house team is duplicating the trades without paying the external manager fees on the invested capital. More importantly, if the in-house management team is not successful in generating consistent alpha, it can be politically difficult to remove the team managing the in-house portfolio.

Structure

As active managers and institutional client needs have evolved, so too have the structures that active managers offer clients. There are active equity managers that invest long only (meaning they do not short equities). Typically, these managers have a fixed management fee and no performance fee. There are specialized active managers that, as a result of proven success, are able to charge both a management fee and a performance fee. There are also directional long/short equity managers that tend to have market beta exposure of 70–90% that almost always charge a management and performance fee. In some cases, the performance fee is charged as a percent above a benchmark (fee on alpha), while in others it is charged on any return above zero. In other words, the performance fees are charged on beta and alpha. The willingness to pay fees is particular to an institution.

At Hewlett, we focus on consistency of returns, net of fees, because we want the General Partner to be aligned in creating value for the portfolio. The difference between returns gross of fees and net of fees tends to be significant and should be considered. We consider the math and assess the confidence we have in the manager's ability to generate alpha consistently to make it worth paying the fees. In the simplest form, fees are a headwind pushing against alpha generation.

Because the Hewlett portfolio does not have inflows of additional capital, we are constantly evaluating potential new investment managers relative to existing managers and other peers. A year ago, we were evaluating whether we should remain invested with a manager charging both management and performance fee (manager A) or invest with a manager charging a fixed management fee (manager B). In evaluating manager A, we had to understand the expected gross alpha the manager would have to generate on an annualized basis to be able to deliver net of fees alpha within our expectations. We had to make sure the portfolio took enough active risk to be able to generate high enough alpha (gross of fees) and ensure the active risk the manager was taking was not concentrated in any sector or market capitalization. The offset was that we had great confidence in manager A's ability to generate consistent alpha. Compare this to manager B, who had a fixed, and relatively low-cost, fee structure. But we had less confidence in their ability to earn consistent alpha net of fees. In the end, we chose to retain our current manager roster and continue meeting with manager B with a clear view of what it would take for us to increase our confidence in their ability to generate consistent alpha. Manager selection criteria and the qualities that lead us to gain confidence in a particular manager are covered in depth in Chapter 12.

Beyond the performance fee, investors have to consider whether the institution is compensated for taking illiquidity risk within public equities. For example, some managers offer only three- or five-year share classes in order to ensure they can implement a thoughtful, long-term investment strategy without facing short-term redemption risks. Other managers may also have significant restrictions on the time it takes to fully redeem. In general, managers create fee structures that incentivize clients to extend lockups through lower manager fees, higher return hurdles, or lower performance fees. It is important to analyze what the break-even point of return is across different share classes in selecting the appropriate asset class for the institution.

Once investors have clarified the role of public equities and considered options for implementing this part of the investment portfolio, the team needs to consider the breadth of market exposures the equity portfolio should include.

- Regional exposures can be implemented using active or passive strategies. There are many ways to think about obtaining regional exposure. It can be U.S. only, or perhaps only developed markets like U.S., Europe, and Japan. Or perhaps there is desire to invest in emerging markets. There are benefits to public equity exposure diversified across geographies with different monetary and economic cycles. When investing outside of the institution's home currency (U.S. dollar), investors need to consider currency risk, since returns of the index are calculated in local currency while the portfolio earns the return in U.S. dollars.

- Sector exposures can also be implemented in active or passive strategies. For example, if an institution has significant exposure to technology in its venture portfolio, then a portfolio could be constructed in a way that excludes technology from the public portfolio. Similarly, if an institution wants exposure to tech innovation but has only begun to commit to venture, then ensuring the appropriate exposure to tech innovation could be easily done through passive instruments.

- Factor exposure typically refers to tilts within a public equity portfolio toward growth, value, or momentum. Over the past 20 years as quantitative strategies have grown, there are strategies employing over 30 different factors. Simple factor strategies, such as growth, value, and momentum, can be implemented using passive funds or ETFs. Complex factor strategies are best implemented by active quantitative managers that have the tools and skill set to trade the factors.

- Market capitalization exposure determines the investment universe of public companies that can be included in the passive or active manager portfolio. ETFs and passive index funds can be low-cost ways of implementing a market capitalization strategy.

At Hewlett, we have a large venture and mid-market buyout port-folio. The underlying portfolio company exposure from the venture and buyout portfolios provides the endowment with exposure to small and mid-capitalization private companies and tilts the exposure of the aggregate equity exposure toward technology. For this reason, the Hewlett public equity portfolio has managers that invest almost en-tirely in large-capitalization companies across a broad set of sectors and geographies. When we look at the underlying exposures of the combined public and private equity portfolio, we have confidence we have the diversification necessary to consistently deliver the goal of generating returns from growth in companies through capital apprecia-tion and dividends.

Nuances of Fixed Income

Fixed income securities can, at times, provide a tactical protective quality to portfolios, since there are periods when equity and bond markets are negatively correlated. While bonds reliably served as a counterbalance to equity risk over the past 20 years, prior decades experienced posi-tive correlation between bond and equity markets (refer to Chapter 5, Figure 5.2). Negative correlation between equity and bonds should not be counted upon as the primary tool in risk management. Fixed income should be judged in absolute terms (the yield) and by how it integrates into the institution's risk framework, in addition to the potential return the asset class generates relative to a benchmark.

The extent to which fixed income can serve as ballast to the eq-uity portfolio is not only based on the correlation assumption, but also on the absolute level of fixed income yields. When absolute yield on fixed income bonds is high, the portfolio is able to earn an acceptable nominal return from the interest/yield of the bond, with the possibility of capital gains if interest rates decline. In contrast, when fixed income yields are close to zero, the portfolio doesn't have the benefit of earning an acceptable nominal yield and has the risk of loss of value if and when interest rates rise. For this reason, the deployment of capital in a portfo-lio to fixed income should vary based on the expected contribution to return and the degree of protection it can potentially offer the portfolio.

Many investors presume it is challenging to generate alpha in fixed income securities; thus institutions focused on alpha generation have tended to allocate only a small portion of their portfolios to fixed income or have made allocations using passive strategies. Notwithstanding, active managers still dominate fixed income markets because active fixed income managers have outperformed passive fixed income strategies that mimic the index. There is a simple explanation for this; the manner in which fixed income indices are constructed differs materially from the construction of equity indices. Equity indices represent 85% of the market capitalization of the equity market; however, the broadest U.S. fixed income index (the Bloomberg US Agg Total Return Index) represents only 50% of outstanding fixed income securities. As such, the opportunity set for active fixed income managers to find attractive opportunities outside of the securities held by the index is significant. Successful active managers today manage portfolios that are differentiated from the index to be able to generate returns, net of fees, above the index.

Most institutions think of fixed income in two buckets: rates and credit. The decision of what type of fixed income to include in the portfolio depends on what the objective is in having fixed income in the portfolio. Whether the role is safety, liquidity, downside protection, or generating cash flow, the selection of the type of bonds to include matters. Similar to equities, investors need to explore how various fixed income instruments can fit into a portfolio that meets their goal.

- Rates (duration): Intermediate-term-duration U.S. Treasuries and agencies are often used to offset equity risk in a portfolio. Value can be added by actively trading duration. Strategic cash in institutional portfolios is typically 2–3% and left in short-term instruments.

- Credit (spread): Public credit vehicles provide equity-like returns typically with half the expected volatility of public equity. Implementation in investment grade (IG), high-yield, commercial mortgage-backed securities (CMBS) and residential mortgage-backed securities (RMBS) provides a differentiated source of return. Markets can become disorderly due to limited liquidity of individual credit issuers. Active managers in fixed income are able to step in and provide liquidity in times when markets overshoot.

- Private credit: Private credit funds allow investors to access a broader universe of debt and often result in more resilient debt structures since the investment firm is negotiating the legal agreement. However, the ability to allocate capital to private credit structures is limited by the degree to which the portfolio is at or near the maximum illiquidity threshold since investing in private credit competes with higher expected return in venture and buyout. For practical reasons, it may be useful to find short-duration private credit that has an objective of generating cash flows and matures within a couple of years.[2]

Investors should demand an illiquidity premium to invest in private credit. Drawdown structures offered by private credit managers prove useful in being able to put money to work during periods of dislocations. Typically, private credit funds charge a management fee on called capital and a performance fee on returns above zero (in other words, the performance fees are charged on beta and alpha). The difference between returns gross of fees and net of fees tends to be significant (though less than private equity and real estate) and should be considered relative to public credit alternatives.

Hedge Funds are an Essential Tool

The most common types of hedge funds are equity long/short, credit long/short, multi-strategy, market neutral, and relative value. Hedge funds have disappointed investors for over a decade due to inconsistent returns and high management and performance fees. The variety of strategies aggregated under the hedge fund umbrella is partly to blame for investor dissatisfaction with the asset class over the past decade. Complicating it further is that hedge fund managers are not quite sure what their limited partners (LPs) want since some LPs may have hired the manager to have less downside capture, while other LPs may have hired the manager to find relative value among various asset classes.

There are periods of years when earning return on full beta exposure turns out to be the right decision, and any hedged exposure means return was left on the table. In addition, investors need to consider that hedge fund fees reduce net return to investors over a multi-year period by a meaningful amount because fees are typically charged at the end of each year. Similar to the considerations in public equity, investors have to consider the illiquidity of various share classes and whether the fee

---

[2] Multiple of invested capital (MOIC) on a credit fund is not as attractive as other illiquid investment funds, but as the capital is returned in a quicker fashion due to cash flow profile, an investor can commit to subsequent funds and compound returns over time in a manner that is able to compete with buyout returns.

structure and redemption terms adequately compensate the endowment for locking up capital for a period of time.

Clarity on the goal is crucial in allocating capital to the asset class and to develop a framework to understand the type of hedge fund strategies appropriate for the portfolio. Some investors want hedge funds to serve as a low-beta strategy within their portfolios. Some investors want to participate in market rallies and seek a completely different return profile from their hedge funds. Perhaps the goal is producing consistent, attractive returns at a much lower market beta than everything else in the portfolio.

- Low-beta: Low-beta strategies are designed to preserve capital and serve as a ballast for equity exposure elsewhere in the portfolio. A low-beta hedge fund portfolio typically has a target beta of 0.2, which leads investors toward relative value, market neutral, and other low-beta strategies. The drawback is that capital is allocated into strategies that have a fairly low and narrow band of potential return.

- Medium-beta: Medium-beta strategies typically have a target beta of 0.3 and are designed to produce returns that are in the mid-single digits but with greater consistency than public equities. The primary exposure within medium-beta strategies is credit given the consistency and different return drivers (see credit section above). Directional credit strategies can be combined with market neutral and other low-beta strategies to protect downside risk.

- Moderate-beta: Moderate-beta strategies have a greater allocation to directional credit strategies, and typically include a healthy allocation to long/short equity hedge funds. While the expected beta is 0.4, at times the realized beta of this type of hedge fund portfolio could be closer to 0.7. Moderate beta strategies make sense for investors focused on maximizing the probability of growing the asset base.

Lastly, I would add that investing in public assets can be implemented using fundamental analysis, technical analysis, or both. Fundamental analysis is preferable for long-term investors since there is valuation work underpinning the investment decision. Being patient (and unemotional) with good and bad investments is easier when investors have done the fundamental detailed work. Technical analysis shortens the time horizon significantly. Once a fundamental decision to invest or sell has been made, technical analysis can be useful as a trading tool.

Hopefully, it is clear that the tool kit provided by public assets comes in handy when developing the policy portfolio. Inasmuch as the lure of private investments pulls investors into increased allocations to private asset classes, the role of different public strategies is critical in active management of an endowment portfolio. Public market returns may be more limited in scope than private markets over a long-term horizon; however, the liquidity and flexibility afforded by public markets cannot be beat.

4

Perspectives on Private Markets

I suspected that each of my teammates hoped as fervently as I that [he]. . . had been careful to weed out clients of dubious ability and would have the means to protect each of us from one another's shortcomings.
—John Krakauer, referring to Rob Hall in *Into Thin Air*[1]

Investment returns can be earned from taking different types of risks. In the prior chapter, we considered the type of return premia that can be earned in liquid, public securities by taking interest rate (duration) risk, credit risk, and public equity risk. Investing in private markets allows investors the opportunity to earn illiquidity risk premia, as well as providing investors the ability to invest in companies not available for investment through public investment vehicles.

As the expedition team settles into base camp and begins to assess the various tools in the team's packs, it is important to assess the necessity and role of every new tool being added. Consider public assets to be the basic tools needed for the ascent (e.g., radios, sunglasses, ropes, ice picks), while private investment asset classes are the specialty tools without which most of us cannot ascend to the summit (e.g., oxygen tanks, crampons). Just as specialty tools are expensive and difficult to use, so too are private investment funds.

---

[1] Jon Krakauer, *Into Thin Air* (New York: Knopf Doubleday Publishing Group, 1998), 40.

The Role of Private Investments

The role of private assets in a diversified portfolio is to provide higher-than-expected returns and diversification relative to public assets. The expectation of higher return incorporates illiquidity premia, as well as compensation for execution risk by both the general partner (GP) and the management teams at the portfolio companies. Often, a portion of the higher expected return in private markets is simply a result of the leverage employed to generate the return.

There are significant advantages to adding private funds to an institutional portfolio. First, being able to own private assets allows the portfolio to have a more complete opportunity set. The structure of public markets has changed over the past 20 years, and there are currently fewer than 4,000 listed public companies compared to 8,000 listed public companies two decades ago. Private assets account for 60% of economic activity and growth not captured in public asset markets. A majority of real estate assets are privately held. By investing in private markets, investors can participate in regions or sectors where there are few public market opportunities. Private asset markets are typically less efficient than public markets and can provide attractive risk-adjusted returns.

Beyond the expanded opportunity set, private investments allow the time and patience to create value through active management of the asset. The GP has time to evaluate new opportunities with access to a significant amount of information and, hopefully, minimize surprises. The GP controls the levers for creating value through repositioning, enhancing the management team, expanding revenue channels, optimizing production, leverage, or vertical integration, just to name a few. Management teams in private companies have the luxury of being able to implement significant change outside the glaring spotlight of quarterly earnings reports. Ideally, this allows private firms to be improved with greater adherence to a well-thought-out strategy and to realize the full potential of the company or asset at exit.

Unlike public markets, private asset markets do not have an investable index to provide exposure to the investment opportunity. Investors are unable to buy the market (beta) exposure. Instead, the market (beta) is a result of the decisions made by thousands of private investment firms. The "market" is defined looking backwards at a pooled mean of all the funds in the asset class. Both in terms of measuring alpha (return in excess of the benchmark) and understanding intended and unintended sector or geographic tilts, investors are limited to looking in the rearview mirror.

Venture Capital

Venture capital is the highest expected-return asset class in most institutional portfolios to compensate for high execution risk and long hold periods. The role of venture equity is to generate returns from participating in innovation and disrupting existing business models. Venture capital serves an important role investing in the companies that will disrupt today's public companies with faster and/or cheaper goods and services. Value is created by providing founders the capital and guidance to help them effectively communicate an idea and have the ability to develop a product or service that can scale to serve a global market.

Returns from venture and distributions back to limited partners (LPs) are episodic and have very large variations among GPs. Execution risk is the highest of any asset class in the endowment. Early-stage venture companies take 8–10 years to exit and are the least sensitive to changes in the external environment. Late-stage venture companies are closer to exit and are more significantly impacted by the capital markets' environment for an exit, either via an IPO or sale to a strategic buyer.

Buyout

The role of buyout is to participate in the revenue and profit growth of the economic power created by privately held firms not captured in public markets. The goal is to create valuable companies that can flourish for decades after the GP exits the investment. The execution risk is high, especially given the leverage used to acquire the portfolio company. Returns are driven by revenue and cash flow growth, enhanced with leverage.

Value creation typically involves broadening the product offering, enhancing revenue opportunities, opening new markets, reducing operating inefficiencies, use of data to inform product development and production facilities, and creating a sustainable and growing source of earnings. Strengthening the management team and improving the human capital at the portfolio companies is an important element for execution of the strategy. For some buyout firms, actively aggregating smaller companies within a subsector and transforming them into an integrated company at scale allows the GP to capture value in the upward valuation of the multiple paid for larger enterprises. The management teams at the portfolio companies have significantly more equity ownership than typical public equity management teams, further aligning the incentives to generate returns for investors.

Real Estate

The role of commercial real estate is to provide a consistent return profile backed by underlying hard assets that can generate current income and return from capital gains from repositioning and stabilizing real estate assets. It is important to define the role in the portfolio; for some it's an asset that can participate in inflation, while for others, real estate's role is to generate equity-like capital gains. Similar to hedge funds, it is critical to be clear on the exact objective of including real estate in the tool kit.

For institutions that want a tool kit that provides some defense against inflationary pressure and a reliable source of cash flow, core real estate fits the need. Core real estate typically consists of fully leased, stabilized assets that distribute cash flows and contribute to generating liquidity for an institution's payout. Returns tend to be similar to what investors earn in public investment-grade bonds. It is unusual for investors to earn much of an illiquidity premium.

Investors that want to participate in secular growth and operational value creation may consider value-add strategies that use leverage to enhance returns. Typically, value-add investments provide little inflation protection since under-leased buildings are unable to benefit from rent increases when there is vacant space. There are two drivers of property price appreciation beyond the transformation: income growth (NOI) and cap rates. NOI is analogous to earnings/dividends growth in equity markets and is expected to keep pace with inflation. Cap rates represent the yield that can be earned on a property (NOI divided by the price of the property). Returns are generally lower than buyout and venture, but real estate provides the portfolio with diversification because returns are not tied to equity beta, although availability of debt capital underpins both the buyout and real estate asset classes.

Value creation by GPs tends to be in identifying property-types where their skill set can improve operations (hospitality and multi-family apartments) or can aggregate assets for large-scale buyers (logistics, studios, etc.). The tool kit for improving operational cash flow tends to include transforming buildings that can be leased at higher rent levels and incorporating new energy and water systems to reduce operating costs. Typically, assets are sold within 24 months of stabilized cash flow.

Real Assets

The role of real assets is being redefined as many institutions incorporate constraints set by the board on making new commitments to oil and gas assets. During this transition, real assets are being defined as a collection of idiosyncratic assets (e.g., pipelines, orchards, toll roads, cell towers, solar farms, etc.) that share the characteristics of having the potential to generate cash flow streams in a consistent manner once stabilized.

GPs create value through identification of secular trends and sourcing operating partners with the skill set required to maximize return from the secular opportunity set. Long-term expected returns are lower than venture and buyout, and are similar to private credit.

The Illiquidity Premium

We will spend a great deal of time in the portfolio-construction and manager-selection chapters exploring execution risk of private assets. However, what is unique to private assets is the illiquidity premium. The illiquidity premium is what an investor expects to be paid for locking up their capital for a period of a decade or more and reducing the flexibility in the endowment. It is important to note that once you invest in private assets you have taken on the illiquidity risk for the duration of the fund life, yet whether LPs are adequately compensated for the illiquidity risk remains to be seen over the life of the investment.

The illiquidity premium an investor expects to earn is not constant and cannot be observed. There are historical long-term averages that can serve as a guide in developing capital market assumptions and designing a policy portfolio. However, investors should be aware that the illiquidity premium demanded by investors is affected by both the external market conditions and the tolerance for illiquidity of each institution.

During periods when monetary policy is accommodative or periods of strong economic growth, the willingness to take additional risk increases. Investors are more willing to incur illiquidity risk in order to earn a higher expected return. As capital flows into private asset markets, the premium investors receive for illiquidity declines. The extent to which illiquidity premia compress varies across private asset classes. The more limited the investment opportunity in an asset class, the greater the compression in illiquidity premium as demand from new capital inflows overwhelms the opportunity set.

Even if there was an observable gauge for the illiquidity premium, it would be of little use during the expedition team's ascent because the premium each team places on liquidity is different. It is different not only because of the illiquidity tolerance of the institution, but also because the closer the institution is to the theoretical or actual maximum illiquidity threshold, the greater the premium any investment needs to have to earn a place in the portfolio.

For example, two institutions have individually arrived at the same conclusion that maximum illiquidity is 35% and the expected return from illiquidity premium is 300 basis points above the expected return of the public assets in the portfolio. The teams are each presented with an opportunity to invest in a new private fund with an expected return that is 300 basis points above the comparable investment in public markets. The decision seems clear in that it meets the expected return hurdle.

However, institution A has a young portfolio where the private portfolio is being built out and private investments are at 20%. Institution B has a mature portfolio that has been built over more than a decade and illiquid investments already compose 35% of the endowment.

The CIO of institution A may approve the investment even if the expected return is a bit below the 300 bp expected illiquidity premium used in the capital market assumptions underpinning the asset class policy allocation. After all, the team is actively looking for opportunities and competing for capacity in sought-after funds. The CIO can consider that over a decade the illiquidity premium will rise and fall, and the expected 300 bp can be earned long term.

On the other hand, the decision is more complex for the CIO at institution B because the institution has little room to grow illiquid investments. The CIO at institution B evaluates each incremental dollar of commitment against the existing illiquid portfolio, expected distributions, and against every other opportunity anticipated for the coming year. Intuitively, the CIO of institution B increases the hurdle of expected return in order to approve the next commitment of capital to an illiquid fund.

Duration of Investment Holding Period

Another factor to consider in allocating capital across private asset classes is expectation of weighted average life (WAL) of the portfolio companies and whether longer holding periods are preferable to LPs. In some cases, portfolio companies are able to compound returns from earnings and dividends at a low teens pace (although this is likely 8% net of fees). In a recent Harvard Business School study on private equity, most firms underwrite cash flows for five years, at which point they calculate a terminal or exit value typically determined by using comparable data on public companies and transactions.

In buyout, real estate, and some real asset strategies, the significant value creation and boost to EBITDA and valuation multiple occurs as soon as the GPs are done building and/or fixing the companies, pipelines, or buildings. The contribution to return is mostly from the heavy lift of restructuring or repositioning the asset in the first three years. Once the asset has been restructured or repositioned, cash flow growth tends to be in the mid-single digits. The longer holding period exposes the investment to traditional "levered beta" factors and diminishes the contribution to return from idiosyncratic factors. One could argue that long holding periods for some private strategies do not make sense, given other options for reinvestment across the portfolio.

In growth strategies, the boost to EBITDA and valuation multiple occurs as accretive add-on acquisitions and operational tool kits expand revenues, customer base, and operational efficiency throughout the period the GP owns the investment. The contribution to return comes mostly from the execution of strategic vision of the management team and the GP. Given high growth rates for many portfolio companies in these strategies, GPs may continue to hold their stakes to benefit from the compounding effect or take advantage of the multiple expansion arbitrage and sell the firm to a larger buyout firm or strategic investor.

Leverage

Traditional buyout and real estate strategies, exemplified by the mega-buyout firms, tend to utilize financial engineering as a core part of their strategy. Typically, traditional buyout and real estate portfolio companies are levered 60–70% (debt-to-total capital). The level of debt in the capital structure varies by industry, given wide dispersion in the volatility of cash flow in cyclical versus non-cyclical sectors. It is also highly related to the price paid, the ability to obtain higher levels of debt when interest rates are low, and whether liquidity is plentiful. Restructuring strategies, by the nature of the complexity and risk, usually have low leverage at purchase, and it is only after the business has been fixed that additional leverage is used. The contribution to return earned by managers from the use of leverage is fairly straightforward to calculate and can be easily incorporated into diligence analysis of the manager.

Traditional Fund Structures

In most institutions, the investment team participates in private market opportunities through private fund structures with a 10- to 12-year life (plus two 1- to 2-year extensions). The institution's capital is commingled with other institutional capital in a limited-liability partnership (LP) structure, and the GP has full discretion over how the capital is invested over a predetermined two-to-five-year investment period. The fund owns the portfolio companies or assets, and the discretion on sale of a business lies entirely with the GP.

The advantages of raising funds every few years are fairly straightforward for the LP since the LP retains the right to re-underwrite the decision at each subsequent fund raise. The LP also retains the flexibility to modify the amount of dollars committed in subsequent funds based on the individual needs of the institution and other opportunities being discussed across the portfolio. Individual fund cycles force accountability for the GP to deliver distributions and returns to the LPs that have provided them with capital to invest.

For the GP there is the burden of taking time away from investing to raise the subsequent fund in order to ensure that the firm's investment team has capital available for any opportunity that may arise. That said, GPs can also benefit from the discipline each fund cycle brings in terms of the allocation of carry in each fund among the GP's partners. Unfortunately, individual fund raises also increase the possibility that the firm may be unable to raise a subsequent fund if they have failed to deliver returns to their LPs.

Alternative Fund Structures

Permanent Capital Vehicles

These vehicles are sometimes referred to as evergreen funds and were created to lessen reinvestment risk for LPs. Instead of committing to individual funds with a GP, the LP commits to a permanent fund vehicle with the expectation that proceeds from sales of assets will be reinvested instead of distributed to LPs. In some cases, the "evergreen" vehicle allows additional contribution of capital once a year or once every few years. Depending on the vehicle, management fee and carry are charged to investors every year (at the time a portfolio company or asset is sold) or every time there is a window for new capital contributions. This compares to traditional private funds where carry is charged after the LP receives full return of their capital contribution, and in some cases, an additional preferred return.

The advantage for the GP is clear. They do not have to spend time fundraising and can devote all of their time to doing what they love to do, investing. They also lock in a fairly sizable recurring revenue stream with which to build the firm, with the resources that can support an ever-growing asset base.

The advantage for LPs is unclear. The CIO loses control of the capital deployed with a single GP since there are no distributions, and as the return compounds, it simply increases the exposure within the portfolio that cannot be actively managed. Evergreen vehicles place little pressure on the GP to implement changes quickly and remove the pressure to exit assets. It is difficult for LPs to discern whether the GP is maximizing the value of any single asset in the fund and whether the internal investment hurdle is being met by older investments.

Co-Investment Vehicles

Co-investment opportunities are presented as special-purpose vehicles (SPVs) created alongside an existing private fund making new investments. These vehicles serve two purposes. First, having this "reserve" pool of capital allows the GP to write equity checks for an asset that is too large for the main fund vehicle. In this case, the LPs can participate by subscribing to the SPV to provide capital in excess of the capital already committed to the main fund. Second, co-invest allows LPs to put capital to work in identified opportunities (as opposed to the fund where the investments have not been identified when the fund is raised). Co-invest typically has more favorable fees, and thus, an LP can lower the overall cost of investment with a GP. Alignment of interests is clear since the SPV will enter and exit the investment at the same time as the main fund.

Continuation Vehicles

Continuation vehicles are a fairly recent tool used by GPs to "lift" a portfolio company or asset out of the main fund into a new special-purpose vehicle or fund structure. Unlike co-investments, where there is alignment of interest and the definition of what constitutes a co-invest is clearly understood, continuation vehicles are a catch-all category. Thus far, we have seen three main uses of CV structures for single assets due to different stages of a portfolio company's life and different stage of GP ownership in the company or asset.

> Fund life constraint: This tends to happen when a portfolio company was bought late into a fund's life and the sweet spot of change (years 3–5) exceeds the remaining life of the fund vehicle. The LP needs to be sure the strategic plan can be executed in the new continuation vehicle, and that the GP carry (if any) is rolled into the new vehicle. The LP should also push the GP to consider accelerating the change strategy and fully utilizing the two fund extension options to exit before the fund life ends. In practice, LPs would prefer to approve several fund life extensions that provide the GP with an acceptable time frame in which to exit the asset.

> New leg of transformational growth: This occurs when the GP believes there is another leg of transformation, but the remaining fund life is too short or the LPs in the main fund are eager for liquidity. In effect, while the GP does have experience with the portfolio company, the CV is starting a new growth trajectory and should be underwritten as a new investment opportunity. Clearly identifying incentives for the GP and the management team ahead of time can serve as useful tools for understanding the growth plan and the strategy for exit.

> Quality compounder: A third type of CV use occurs when a company is stabilized and compounding returns at mid-teens, and the GP is reluctant to sell the company or asset because the GP and some LPs prefer to compound return. The CV provides liquidity for LPs that want to exit and reduces execution and reinvestment risk for LPs who participate in the CV.

The advantage of CVs for LPs is that there is a liquidity event in the main fund that "sells" the company or asset to the continuation vehicle. If the LP wants to continue its ownership, the LP can elect to roll all or part of the investment in a tax-efficient manner into the continuation vehicle. An LP can also choose to receive a full distribution of its interest. Since the participants in a CV are usually not identical to the LPs in the main fund, there is a third-party valuation that is used to determine the price at which the transaction between the main fund and the CV occurs.

More recently, CVs have expanded from single asset to portfolios of assets held by a single or multiple funds. In these transactions, the GP selects individual portfolio companies from one or more of their funds and contributes the assets into a new SPV. Typically, one of the GP's large institutional investors has committed to participate and provide liquidity to LPs opting to sell. In some cases, a new provider of capital (not an existing LP) will commit to purchase the pool of assets using third-party valuation to determine the price.

In both single-asset and portfolio-of-assets CVs, the GP gets to take its carry at the point of the exit from main fund. If the GP does not roll its carry into the CV, then LPs should be concerned about misalignment of interest. After all, the GP retains the active management of the company or asset but is no longer as incentivized as LPs to generate superior returns since their carry has been crystallized.

Table 4.1 has a list of things for CIOs to consider when using co-investment or other types of structures as part of the tools on the ascent to the summit.

Table 4.1

Considerations for Alternative Fund Structures
• Does the investment team have the necessary experience to underwrite each SPV opportunity that is presented?
• Will the team participate in every opportunity for co-investment, or will the team cherry-pick co-investment opportunities?
• Is co-investment a structural strategy within an asset class?
• Will SPV participation be limited only to existing managers in the portfolio where there is an ongoing relationship?
• Do you demand a higher expected return for a co-invest than you would for the main fund since there is single asset risk?
• Over what time frame will performance be measured?

Source: The William and Flora Hewlett Foundation.

Reconciling Performance

Private investment funds typically charge a management fee every year plus a percentage of the profits the GP generates on the capital invested by the LP. The standard fee is 2% management fee to pay for the team, the infrastructure, the cost of doing business, and so on. The carry can vary between 15% and 30% depending on the asset class, vehicle type, distribution waterfall, and the bargaining power of the GP.[2] The mechanism for calculating carry can make a material difference in the net returns received by an LP and the return the GP believes they generated for the LP (the gross return).

Investors should spend time reconciling the "top-down" expected return for each private asset class, with the "bottom-up" expected return of each fund underwritten by the investment team. Top-down expected return calculations use time-weighted return (TWR)[3] methodology and incorporate cross-cycle, net-of-fees returns. Top-down return expectations represent the asset class, not the collection of managers in whom the institution has invested or committed capital. Top-down expected returns, net of fees, for private asset class range from 7% to 12% depending on the asset class and institution. However, institutional investors typically underwrite new private fund commitments to a "hurdle" internal rate of return of 15% to 25% net of fees.

The reconciliation between top-down and bottom-up involves three main adjustments: investing through the cycle, duration of the investment, and fees. First, top-down expected return is calculated using TWR and assumes investing in the asset class through cycles, with both good and bad vintages. Conversely, the expected return on a bottom-up basis reflects the GP's base case for internal rate of return (IRR)[4] without incorporating expectations of return if there is a recession, period of closed capital markets, or mis-execution of strategy. In addition, the top-down expected return is net of all fees and carry, resulting in a wide gap from underwritten gross returns on a bottom-up basis. The gross/net difference in return significantly reduces the expected return earned by an LP. In good years, LPs may receive 50–65% of the gross return reported by a fund after management fees and carry. Albeit, in bad vintage years, the gross/net difference is reduced, since there is only the management fee to serve as a drag on returns received by an LP.

To illustrate the concept of "investing through full cycle," see Table 4.2. The portion of capital-weighted average life (WAL) between

---

[2] Carry can be calculated using an American waterfall (deal-by-deal basis) or a European waterfall (on fund basis). European waterfall is LP-friendly because the GP will not earn carry until all LP capital and preferred return have been fully distributed.

[3] Return assumptions are time-weighted, geometric, nominal, and exclude potential alpha.

[4] Internal rate of return (IRR) is the calculation of return on an investment assuming reinvestment of cash flows at the same rate of return of the investment.

Table 4.2

	Portion of capital-weighted WAL in good VYs	Return in good VYs	Return in bad VYs	Total return
Venture	60%	18%	3%	12%
Buyout	60%	15%	8%	12%
Real estate	50%	13%	3%	8%
Natural resources	50%	13%	3%	8%

Source: The William and Flora Hewlett Foundation. Burgiss data 2004–2019.

good and bad vintage years is based on the benchmark return of each private asset class from 2004 to 2019. In summary, venture and buyout have a greater portion of capital-weighted WAL in good vintage years (60%) as opposed to real estate and natural resources (50%). Importantly, the return in good vintage years of venture and buyout was also greater than good vintage years in real estate and natural resources. For example, vintage year analysis for real estate shows that in good vintage years the return of the benchmark was 13%, while in bad vintage years it was 3%. On a weighted basis, through a full cycle the return was 8%.

Measuring the absolute performance of a GP is straightforward, since the LP's custodian and investment operations team receive capital account statements detailing the change in value and any flows (calls and distributions) every quarter. The LP reports the change in value in its financial accounts alongside the returns of public investments. There are two things to consider in analyzing performance. The capital account statements typically do not deduct the earned (but unpaid) GP carry allocation. It is also important to take into account the degree to which the performance in a fund has been realized or remains largely unrealized.

GPs tend to measure their success in terms of gross returns. Many present gross returns in marketing materials and LP updates, yet the LP only earns returns after management fee, carry, and taxes have been charged. In the case of international investments, GPs often present returns gross of foreign exchange losses and tax withholding.

For example, many years ago Hewlett underwrote an opportunity to invest in distressed real estate in Japan in a typical fund structure with 2% management fee and 20% carry. On the surface, the gross return hurdle being used by the GP presented a compelling risk-reward investment for us. After months of due diligence, we gained strong conviction in the GP and believed that the opportunity set was robust. However, as the team began to peel the layers of foreign taxes, currency, fees, and carry waterfall, the return opportunity became much less compelling relative to the risk of execution of the strategy. As such, we opted not to invest because our objective is to deliver superior risk-adjusted returns net of all fees and taxes. In hindsight, we know the fund generated strong gross and net returns and was able to execute the intended strategy. We don't get every decision right, and that is okay as long as we followed our process for making decisions.

Part II

THE EXCITEMENT OF THE CLIMB

From Base Camp to First Camp

The climb from base camp to first camp is a strenuous and challenging trek crossing glaciers and navigating crevasses that requires planning and execution to ensure that the expedition team remains safe. The decision to invest time in identifying the summit and developing a policy portfolio is separate from the decision to implement the expedition plan. Between base camp and first camp the expedition team has one objective: to develop a policy portfolio that meets the needs of the organization and is flexible enough to withstand the uncertainties that will be faced on the way to the summit.

The expedition team has the technical skills to navigate the challenges, yet the process is time-consuming and tiring. Asset allocation may feel like a significant undertaking, just like crossing the glacier. It is best handled by having patience and making sure everyone is on firm footing. Taking into consideration the return expectations and constraints of the institution, the investment team can design a strategic asset allocation policy that has a level of risk appropriate to generate an expected long-term annualized return. The time spent preparing for base camp and then settling in at base camp should have acclimated the team and the institution to the challenge ahead.

Developing a policy portfolio is challenging because assumptions on which the models are built feel like loose rocks on a narrow ridge and the team has to be careful not to slip or lose their footing. My advice is don't focus on the gravel as you climb toward the ridge and hold on to the fixed ropes in creating the policy portfolio. Similar to the effort that must be made to cross steep sections of the climb toward first camp, testing and considering alternative paths can be helpful in gaining confidence that the path chosen to the summit is the best course available for the institution and possible for the expedition team to survive.

Arriving at first camp, defined as developing, recommending, and having the policy portfolio approved, will feel terrific and allow the team to pause and regain strength. Arriving on a broad, flat ridge with stunning views of the surrounding mountains provides a well-deserved break and helps the expedition team get used to the altitude. The team needs to protect against the elements and keep in mind that the policy portfolio is a road map (not a straitjacket) with sufficient flexibility for the CIO to shift exposure in the portfolio on a tactical basis. Market conditions ebb and flow, requiring shifts in allocation of capital across the various asset classes.

5

Developing a Policy Portfolio

You never climb the same mountain twice, not even in memory. Memory rebuilds the mountain, changes the weather, retells the jokes, remembers all the moves.

—Lito Tejada-Flores[1]

Whether the CIO has inherited an existing portfolio, or has the benefit of building a new portfolio, the CIO and the investment team must develop a policy portfolio to serve as the guide to achieve the investment objective of the organization. A multi-asset class investment program presupposes that the opportunity set in any asset class and geography ebbs and flows over time. Multi-asset class portfolios have flexibility to adapt to changes in the market environment, so long as the team is experienced and has the skills necessary to execute the plan.

For CIOs inheriting a portfolio, the exercise of developing fresh capital market assumptions (CMAs) and analyzing the existing, inherited portfolio using fresh CMAs can provide useful insight into the direction they may want to take in shaping the portfolio for the future.

Many institutional investors use a mean-variance optimization (MVO) model to identify efficient asset allocations. MVO relies on a

---

[1] Lito Tejada-Flores, "Games Climbers Play," *Ascent*, 1967.

series of key inputs and constraints, and provides a number of "optimal" portfolios with target weights per asset class. The optimal portfolio maximizes return at a specific level of volatility (or, conversely, minimizes volatility at a specific expected return).

Capital Market Assumptions

There are three primary sets of capital market assumptions (CMAs) investors must consider to serve as inputs into a mean-variance optimizer used to arrive at an asset allocation policy. There are many ways investors can arrive at expected returns. There is no one way to do this, and definitely no right answer. Accepting that we have no idea what the path of returns will be over a 10-year period is really okay. Think of the mountain analogy; there is so much out of our control, there is no way to know if we will be correct or wrong. Despite this, it is essential to have a plan for the ascent and the descent from the summit so the team can anticipate what comes next. In this way, when the market/weather turns our path into a hazard, we know how to find our way back onto the intended path.

Finally, it is important to consider that CMAs reflect expected return and volatility of the market (beta), not the expected return of an actively managed portfolio with the opportunity to earn alpha (return in excess of the market). In other words, the model needs to be based on the expected return and volatility of each asset class and does not include hoped-for alpha generation.

Expected Return

Since capturing the return available from risk premia is an essential part of the climb, the CIO and team need to agree on a core philosophy on risk premia that will be used to develop the policy portfolio. The hard part is that risk premia are invisible to the eye. The higher you climb, the thinner the air, and the more difficult it is to focus on something intangible.

One key thing that I learned when I started at Hewlett is that the absolute numbers used for the expected risk premia are much less important than how you think about the risk premium of one asset class relative to another. I needed a visualization of this intangible concept. My son was about four when I struggled through my first asset allocation policy exercise. We loved building Legos together. One day sitting on the floor of his room, I started thinking about risk premia and stacking Legos. The analogy is not perfect because unlike Lego blocks, risk premia are not all the same height, and they also expand and compress.

Think of expected return of each asset class as a stack of Lego blocks of many colors. Each color represents a different type of risk premia. Figure 5.1 shows the components of risk premia for each asset class. The risk-free rate is the first Lego block of each stack. For the expected return of fixed income, you add the risk premia of duration to the risk-free rate. For the expected return of credit, you have the risk-free block, plus duration risk premium, plus credit risk premium. Then you start the equity blocks. The expected return of public equity starts with risk-free, then adds equity risk premium. Private assets have an additional block for the illiquidity premium. When you visualize it this way, the risk premia and expected return for each asset class will, hopefully, make a lot more sense.

Without a doubt, developing CMAs by asset class is a process of "informed guesswork." For public asset classes, the "size" of the Lego block or risk premium can be informed by decades of monthly data. While the assumptions may turn out not to be correct, the process by which you arrived at the expected risk premium is prudent. Developing CMAs for private assets presents a different set of challenges because private asset benchmarks are published quarterly. It takes 12 years of private fund data to gather the 60 data points that most statisticians recommend as the minimum number of data points from which to draw any conclusions.

The challenge of using data gathered over the past 15 years, when monetary and fiscal policy was extraordinary, just underscores the point that the assumptions of expected return used in the optimizer are useful guides, not promised returns. It may be useful to compare data sets from

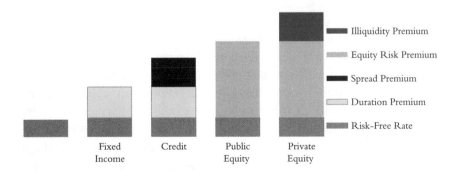

Figure 5.1 Risk Premia
Source: The William and Flora Hewlett Foundation.

prior periods to get a sense of the impact of extraordinary policies. For example, compare the realized return, volatility, and correlation data from 1990 to 2005, against the data set from 2008 to 2023, in developing CMAs.

Many institutional portfolios have an asset class designated Opportunistic Investments. Typically, these are investments that do not fall neatly into the return or risk profile of traditional asset classes. Since these are, by their very nature, idiosyncratic investment opportunities, developing CMAs can be challenging. One suggestion is to assign a blended expected return and volatility based on the underlying factors of expected return. If the investments are "moon shots," then CMAs are likely to be more extreme than CMAs for venture. If opportunistic investments are direct investments in private firms, then CMAs likely resemble buyout CMAs.

Expected Volatility

Fortunately, realized volatility for public asset classes is easy to observe. The team can develop expected volatility assumptions for each asset class using a combination of 20 years of monthly data in public assets and adjusting for the past 15 years of dampened volatility resulting from monetary accommodation.

For private asset classes, the reported marks in privates are smoothed over a quarter and the marks in private assets change more gradually than public markets. In developing expected volatility assumptions for the policy portfolio, investors should look at the underlying risk of each private asset class and not at the realized volatility of the benchmark, because realized volatility of the benchmark will significantly under-represent the risk inherent in the portfolio.

The expected volatility of the asset classes will form the base of the risk models used to manage the portfolio over the long term. The closer they are to representing the true underlying risk of the portfolio, the more effective the risk management tools will be.

At Hewlett, we take a holistic approach to developing expected volatility assumptions for private asset classes. Our objective is to capture the expected contribution to portfolio risk. For example, we believe the underlying volatility risk of buyout is similar to the volatility exhibited by the levered S&P Index. For private credit, we blend bond and equity volatility to arrive at expected volatility. In venture capital, we assume a high degree of volatility given the episodic nature of the asset class. Private real estate is probably the toughest private asset class for which to figure out expected volatility since the underlying risk varies widely depending on the strategy the CIO and director plan to implement in the portfolio. If the strategy for the asset class is largely cash-flow-oriented and backed by buildings, then expected volatility is likely to be similar to private credit. However, if the asset class is expected to be opportunistic and making equity investments in real estate, then the expected volatility would be closer to buyout.

Expected Correlations

Correlations are not static and change over time, as seen on Figure 5.2. Since a correlation matrix needs to be part of any well-thought-out asset allocation exercise, the team also needs to develop long-term correlation assumptions. This can be particularly tricky if there have been a number of years where conditions have been significantly altered by exogenous factors, such as a pandemic or massive fiscal or monetary policy actions. We live in interesting times, and for practical reasons elongating the time period in the data to 20-year correlations is probably the best course of action.

The most important correlations to determine for the asset allocation policy is whether fixed income (U.S. Treasuries) is positively or negatively correlated to risk assets. For most of the past two decades, bonds and equities have been negatively correlated. During the 1990s equities and bonds were almost always positively correlated.[2]

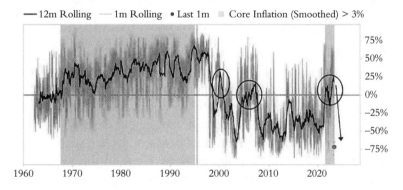

Figure 5.2 Rolling Correlation of Daily Stock and Bond Returns
Source: Bridgewater Associates, 2023, reproduced with permission.

---

[2]Times when investors have experienced negative correlations are during periods of monetary accommodation. We know correlations were negative in 1995 and 1998 for a couple of months after the Tequila and Asian crises. Correlations turned negative when the Fed lowered rates after the tech bubble burst in 2001.

The expected volatility and correlation assumptions underpin the risk models used to manage the portfolio on an ongoing basis. It is important that the investment team dedicate as much time to arriving at these assumptions as they typically spend on expected return assumptions. (See Table 5.1.)

Table 5.1

Considerations in Developing CMAs
• Correlations between bonds and equities
• Correlation between public equity and buyout
• Illiquidity premium across several private asset classes
• The differential in expected return in each asset class relative to other asset classes
• True underlying volatility of private asset classes

Source: The William and Flora Hewlett Foundation.

Optimizer Constraints

Mean-variance optimization models help to identify the asset class mix with the highest expected return at a variety of relevant volatility levels. Plotting the output from each portfolio results in the efficient frontier, or a line representing the highest possible return we could expect to achieve for a given level of risk. While all portfolios on the efficient frontier are, in theory, "optimal," the vast majority would not satisfy both the return needs (returns high enough to maintain or grow inflation-adjusted spending) and risk preferences (minimize chances of large drawdowns) of a typical investment program.

Every mean-variance optimization exercise includes a number of constraints to improve the quality of the output. The constraints are meant to prevent the model from generating portfolios that are unrealistic or unimplementable. As these constraints are self-imposed, each organization should detail each constraint that is used and explain the rationale and impact. Each constraint generally lowers the efficient frontier and should therefore be made with a clear and defensible rationale. There are three primary areas that are often constrained: illiquidity, gross exposure, and asset class exposure.

Every institution has a tolerance for illiquidity and leverage that takes into consideration many factors reviewed in Chapter 1. Less obvious are the limitations on asset class exposures. It is wise to avoid overly narrow asset class categories since the opportunity set shifts over time and the portfolio benefits from having greater flexibility afforded by broad asset class CMAs. For example, the manager universe for an asset class may be insufficiently deep, as was the case for absolute return and venture capital in the past. An asset class may lack the consistency of returns needed to justify a very large allocation (i.e., it may suffer from multi-year dry periods, so should be kept below a certain size), as was the case for real estate and venture capital in the past. An asset class may provide value not captured in a mean-variance framework, such as the value of flexibility provided by holding cash as a permanent allocation in a policy portfolio.

Investment programs shifting from traditional public bond and equity allocations into new, alternative asset classes can capture significant benefits from embracing an endowment portfolio approach. Institutions who are early in the development of their allocation to alternative investments have the opportunity to significantly improve the efficiency of their portfolio asset mix as they shift from the 70/30 equity/bond mix. However, for portfolios that are already diversified into hedged strategies and private asset classes, there are limited ways to further optimize the asset class mix. Instead, efforts are focused on the strategies and tilts implemented within the asset classes themselves, as well as manager selection.

By design, MVO portfolio models assume the portfolio is fully invested at all times. If the organization has a preference for absolute return instead of relative return, then cash becomes an attractive alternative asset class to investing during periods where attractive risk-adjusted opportunities are lacking.

Implications of Constraints

In the example we show in Figure 5.3, we are using the optimizer to identify portfolio asset mixes that maximize return (geometric) at an estimated portfolio volatility of 14%. In this example, the CMAs for buyout result in a lower Sharpe Ratio than other private asset classes to show how a constrained optimizer works. We start with the unconstrained portfolio and layer in each constraint one at a time to quantify the impact of these constraints and hopefully demonstrate their value in the process.

- Unconstrained: In the unconstrained optimization, the expected return of 8.4% looks attractive; however, the model has chosen a portfolio with only five asset classes: 41% allocated to absolute return, 30% to venture capital, 27% to real estate, and 2% to buyout, in addition to the levered 14% fixed income exposure. Private, illiquid asset classes

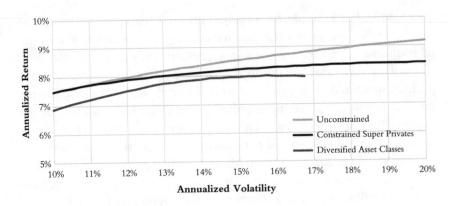

Figure 5.3 Efficient Frontiers
Source: The William and Flora Hewlett Foundation, July 2019.

represent 59% of the portfolio. An unconstrained model will allocate the highest amount to asset classes assumed to have the highest expected Sharpe Ratios. The lack of diversification of asset classes makes the output impractical given the needs of the organization.

- Constrained Private Asset Classes: For reasons detailed in Chapter 4 on the role of private asset classes and their impact on liquidity management, in this example we set a target for private asset class exposure at 38%. When adding this as a constraint, the expected return falls to 8.1% (30 bps lower than unconstrained) as public assets gain share within the mix. The optimizer reduces real estate exposure by 18 percentage points (ppts) to 9%, buyout by 2 ppts to 0%, and venture by 1 ppt to 29%. The optimizer adds 25 ppts to public equity (to 25%) and reduces absolute return by 5 ppts to 36%. While volatility is unchanged, the equity beta rises. Notably, there are still five asset classes without an allocation – credit, bonds, cash, buyout, and natural resources. The private exposure falls within the constraint, but this portfolio is lacking in diversification. This makes the portfolio especially reliant on the accuracy of inputs, or capital market assumptions, which we know to be approximations subject to estimation error.

- Diversified Asset Classes: We add maximum sizes for each asset class to ensure the sources of portfolio beta are diversified. For example, we set a maximum size of 20% for venture, and 15% each for absolute return and real estate. We also add a minimum size for bonds and cash of 3% and 2%, respectively, so that we have one year of payout in liquid, low-risk assets. The impact of these constraints is to further reduce the expected return to 7.9% but provides a portfolio mix with 7.9% expected annualized return (20 bps lower than Constrained Privates), and a diversified, sensible, and investable asset allocation.

The Cloud of Efficiency

While a portfolio below the efficient frontier line is theoretically suboptimal compared to an unconstrained portfolio on the efficient frontier line, most experienced CIOs caution against such a dogmatic interpretation of the efficient frontier. Given the need to incorporate qualitative and subjective factors into the process, as well as the uncertainty levels around model inputs, it is more practical to think of the efficient frontier more as a "cloud" of similarly efficient portfolios near the line that both satisfy efficiency requirements as measured through a mean-variance framework and the individual institution's subjective judgment.

The point of referring to the "cloud" is that there is no one, perfect portfolio once you have built a diversified portfolio. There are subjective trade-offs between the various portfolios, but whether you allocate or reduce 2–4 ppts to an asset class does not move either expected return or risk dramatically. Asset allocation shifts marginally improve expected return or reduce expected risk (probability of a large drawdown), and the room for improvement is small.

Figure 5.4 provides an example of six constrained optimized portfolios (labeled policy through E). The plot shows the efficient "cloud"

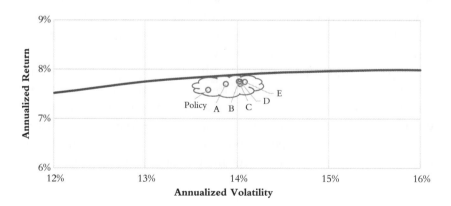

Figure 5.4 Cloud of Efficiency
Source: The William and Flora Hewlett Foundation, July 2019.

of portfolios along the portion of the efficient frontier. Not surprisingly, both the policy portfolio and the other optimized portfolios are within the "cloud" of efficiency.

There are reasons to conduct a comprehensive asset allocation exercise every year or so when the institution's budget is set using the output as a variable, or when an investment program is in its early days. However, experienced CIOs with mature portfolios understand that the cloud of efficiency in asset mix changes and prefer to generate alpha by focusing the energy of the team on manager selection and strategic tilts within the asset classes. Portfolio construction, risk management, and manager selection are the areas when a truly excellent investment team distinguishes itself from the rest of the climbers.

Creating the Policy Portfolio

Once the investment team arrives at the long-term normalized risk premiums, expected return, expected volatility, and expected correlations for the coming decade, the mean-variance optimizer produces a series of potential policy portfolios. Referring back to the Lego analogy in Figure 5.1, the policy portfolio weights can be used to calculate the expected risk premia for the diversified portfolio.[3]

Taking the range of possibilities into consideration and the specific risk profile of the organization, the CIO determines which policy portfolio should be recommended for IC approval for the coming years. It is important to remember that the optimizer does not take liquidity into account when choosing among various asset classes, and the CIO must use judgment in determining the appropriate level of illiquidity across a cycle. Figure 5.5 shows how each asset class fits relative to each other in terms of expected return and volatility risk.

Typically, proposed changes to the policy portfolio are modest because the investment team likes the portfolio they have created, and the risk level is appropriate to achieve the investment objective. The team has confidence in the roster of managers' ability to generate excess returns. In practice, the policy portfolio needs to be modified if the board changes priorities and implements restrictions on investment in

---

[3]The expected risk premia of the diversified portfolio are the sum of the product of the policy weight of an asset class times the risk premium of the asset class.

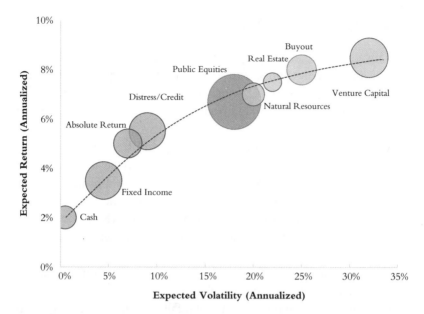

Figure 5.5 Asset Class Expected Return and Volatility Risk
Source: The William and Flora Hewlett Foundation, July 2019.

certain areas (e.g., oil and gas), or directs the team to change the investment process to include non–investment factors.

However, if a CIO inherits a portfolio that is not optimal, it is likely the changes to the policy portfolio will be significant. Conversations with the IC regarding the perceived advantages of moving toward a new policy portfolio can be tricky since the IC presumably approved the policy portfolio being effectively set to one side. In these cases, providing data-based evidence of institutions with similar policy portfolios could be helpful. If the IC resists shifting the policy portfolio in the direction proposed by the CIO, then the CIO may be able to move closer to the efficient frontier through portfolio construction and manager selection in each asset class.

Factors to consider in adjusting the policy portfolio:

- Efficient use of volatility risk budget – e.g., reduce public equities to allow the room in the risk budget for higher venture capital allocation
- Efficient use of the illiquidity risk budget – e.g., increase allocations to privates based on success in securing allocations in funds raised by top-tier venture, buyout, and real estate firms

Range of Possible Outcomes

As the investment team develops capital market assumptions, determines the appropriate constraints, and considers the output of the mean-variance optimizer, the CIO must determine whether the proposed policy portfolio has a high likelihood of achieving the desired objective of the IC and board.

Typically, assumptions about asset class correlations and volatility result in a wide range of possible returns over a short period of time (one to two years). Over a 10-year period, the range of possible outcomes narrows materially, and the spread between the best and worst likely outcomes can actually be quantified. Bear in mind, however, that these are just predictions based on aggregate data and the model is only useful to the extent that the past proves useful in predicting the future.

It is important that the CIO make every effort to communicate with the board that despite careful modeling, the CIO cannot say with certainty where the endowment return will fall within the expected return ranges in any given year; nor can the model predict the timing of any fluctuations up or down. The best the CIO can do is explain that over a decade, the average annualized return for the whole period should be in the target range. In practice, being able to provide the probability of returns in any given year falling into an expected range is enough to provide the organization with the direction needed to plan the main activities of the institution.

Stress Testing

Once the optimizer suggests an appropriate policy portfolio, the investment team must test the policy to be able to convey to the IC and board the probability of achieving the investment objective. The most practical way to do this is to use Monte Carlo simulations to provide guidance for the conversation.

A Monte Carlo simulation is simply a computational process used to approximate the probability of certain outcomes. The process involves running multiple simulations using random variables, and then measuring and tallying the results of each simulation. It is typical to run 100,000 simulations for each portfolio policy mix being considered.

In discussing the downside risks there are two primary hazards that can be modeled. The first risk to consider is the risk of a sharp market correction in any given year or slow protracted drawdown in the value of the endowment. The second hazard to model is the risk that spending needs plus inflation exceeds the portfolio's returns, with the result that spending "eats" into the endowment corpus – reducing inflation-adjusted spending power over time and placing the objective of perpetuity in jeopardy.

The consequences of a significant correction in financial markets are magnified by a combination of inflation and the organization's desire to fund spending. Assume, for example, that the NAV of a portfolio declined by 20% and there were no inflows of capital or donations. This would, in fact, represent a much larger decrease in its inflation-adjusted value, because the organization still has to account for spending (5% in this example) and for inflation. Put in other words, a 20% decline in portfolio returns results in a real (inflation-adjusted) decline of 27% in the overall value of the portfolio (20% decline in NAV + 5% payout + 2% inflation).

Now consider a decline that on the surface appears more benign, say, 2% decline in NAV in year 1 followed by 4% decline in year 2 with no inflows of capital. By funding spending of 5% from the portfolio during years when the endowment is unable to generate a return higher than the level of payout, the endowment is eroded over time. On the surface, this modest correction in the value of the endowment seems manageable and perhaps not worthy of an adjustment in spending. Yet, over the two-year period the combination of funding payout and modestly negative returns results in a decline of 20% in the NAV and granting capacity of the organization.

Table 5.2 illustrates what happens to a hypothetical portfolio at different rates of return in nominal and inflation-adjusted (real) terms.

Table 5.2 Preserving Purchasing Power

Return Assumption		Size of endowment ($B) Real (inflation-adjusted)			Size of payout ($M) Real (inflation-adjusted)		
Nominal	Real	2018	2028	2038	2018	2028	2038
1.0%	−1.0%	9.6	5.2	2.8	470	250	140
3.0%	1.0%	9.6	6.4	4.3	470	310	210
5.0%	3.0%	9.6	7.9	6.4	470	380	310
7.0%	5.0%	9.6	9.6	9.6	470	470	470
9.0%	7.0%	9.6	11.7	14.3	470	570	700

Source: The William and Flora Hewlett Foundation, July 2019.

The highlighted line is a base case scenario: a 7% expected annualized nominal return in an environment of 2% long-term average inflation with 14% volatility and disciplined spending policy of 5%. In real (inflation-adjusted) terms, the portfolio needs to take the risk necessary to generate an expected long-term return of at least 7% nominal (5% real) to maintain the purchasing power of the capital needs of the organization.

To fully appreciate the challenge in determining the appropriate risk level for an organization, consider two points. First, when we talk about "the probability of a drawdown," we are referring to uncertainty around when a significant decline in net asset value may occur and how large it could be, but not whether a drawdown will happen. A drawdown is certain, given the necessity of assuming risk to achieve high enough long-term returns to preserve the endowment's real value over time. Given the level of risk institutions need to accept to achieve average annualized returns of 6–8% over time, market corrections are all but certain to occur at least once during the tenure of a board member.

Figures 5.6 and 5.7 are useful tools for communication between a CIO and the IC and board. In this example, we use a hypothetical portfolio with expected return of 7% and expected volatility of 14%. As you can see in Figure 5.6, the probability of a 21% correction over any particular one-year period is relatively small at 2%. However, Figure 5.7 shows that the probability of a 20% decline increases materially over a longer time horizon.

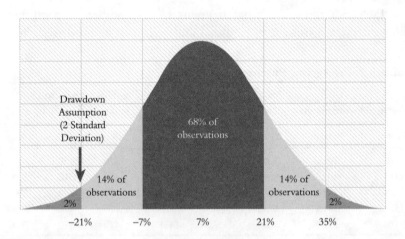

Figure 5.6 Distribution of Returns of Sample Portfolio
Source: The William and Flora Hewlett Foundation, July 2019.

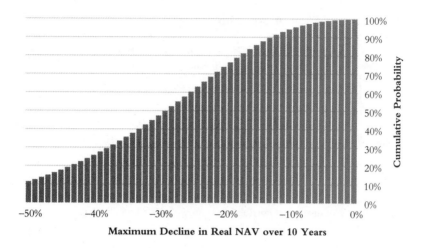

Figure 5.7
Source: The William and Flora Hewlett Foundation, July 2019.

Monte Carlo simulations[4] are useful to understand the probabilities of potential outcomes of a policy portfolio. If we revisit the example of different investment program approaches considered in Chapter 1, and run a Monte Carlo simulation, we can consider the probability of achieving certain goals. An investor could construct the portfolio conservatively to minimize short-term volatility and drawdown risk. This would reduce the near-term threat of a decline in portfolio value, but only by also reducing the expected return below the 5% inflation-adjusted payout. This would likely result in a decline in spending power over time. As a matter of practice, then, most investors choose to accept some short-term volatility to minimize the long-term risk of declining real value.

Table 5.3 provides the probability of achieving the real (inflation-adjusted) spending objective over 10 and 20 years of each of the four portfolio approaches considered in Chapter 1. The model shows the median real net asset value of the portfolio over the same time periods under different portfolio approaches. Importantly, the model provides the probability of a negative cumulative return over any three-year period.

It is challenging to create a model that adequately captures real-world market conditions in a mathematical relationship, especially because

---

[4]A Monte Carlo simulation is a computer algorithm that uses random sampling to provide the likelihood of a range of results happening.

Table 5.3 Comparison of Portfolio Approaches

	70/30 portfolio	High income	Risk parity	Endowment model
Monte Carlo simulation results				
Probability of achieving inflation-adjusted spending objective				
10 YR	40%	30%	48%	60%
20 YR	31%	20%	43%	61%
Median real NAV of diversified portfolio (beginning NAV $7.4 billion)				
10 YR	6.3	5.8	7.0	8.0
20 YR	5.4	4.6	6.5	8.4
Probability of at least one 20% decline in real spending from a previous peak				
10 YR	50%	56%	36%	37%
20 YR	82%	87%	69%	67%
Probability of a negative cumulative return over any 3-year period				
10 YR	65%	68%	49%	56%
20 YR	90%	91%	76%	83%

Source: The William and Flora Hewlett Foundation.

every relationship in the model represents a dynamic system. All models have shortcomings. Models simply cannot include all details and must be overlaid with judgment. Table 5.4 summarizes some of the most glaring

Table 5.4

Shortcomings of the Models

- The model is highly dependent on inputs.
- MVO does not take into account time horizon and assumes the portfolio is the same every year.
- MVO assumes constant rebalancing, even if impractical or costly to do so.
- The model assumes that all risk premia across every asset class rise and fall together at the same time over the 10-year period. In reality, this is unrealistic since capital shifts across assets opportunistically during a 10-year period.
- The models are sensitive to an increase in risk-free rate as the base rate to which investors expect to earn the aggregate risk premia.
- The time-varying DDM methodology is sensitive to increases in the discount rate and the pace of reversion to the mean.

Source: The William and Flora Hewlett Foundation.

shortcomings of models. I highlight these shortcomings as a reminder that models and policy portfolios are useful and necessary guides for the ascent to the summit, yet are unlikely to anticipate the challenges faced on the journey. The IC and the board should understand that the plan will be adapted along the way.

From First Camp to Second Camp

The climb from first camp to second camp is technically challenging and requires both skills and endurance. Although the distance between first and second camps is shorter than between base and first camp, by the time the expedition team successfully arrives at second camp, everyone is exhausted. Active portfolio management also requires skills and endurance. There are steep and rocky sections that must be overcome while facing high winds and extreme cold. There are times when flatter areas of snow and ice will provide the team with a breather and allow everyone to regain strength.

It is in the ascent to second camp that the team gains confidence in the tools packed and food rations, and the bonds deepen among the team and Sherpas. Between first camp and second camp the Sherpas have fixed the ropes, and the team is finding ways to overcome hurdles. This is also the stage where, if systems and necessary infrastructure were not thoughtfully planned, they begin to strain. The higher elevation and stress begin to affect the team in various ways. It is important to take the time to observe if someone is not feeling quite right or if someone is showing signs of buckling under pressure. Given the intensity required to continue, many climbers and investors turn back somewhere before reaching second camp. Turning back requires energy and courage. The expedition leader must help them focus on everything learned up to that point so they can find a new adventure and thrive.

At higher altitude, the complexity of the climb intensifies. Markets surprise even the most experienced investors and as the team moves to higher elevations, everyone needs to be prepared to circumvent an icy waterfall along the way. Sometimes changing conditions appear in the form of a quick bear market sell-off, and sometimes suddenly the skies darken when governance priorities at the institution change. The point is that the team will be surprised and the CIO needs to adjust the plan and ensure that the investment program survives. Importantly, the CIO needs to remain calm and ensure that every member of the expedition team traverses the hazards safely and remains engaged to trek on.

Successful climbers need to always keep in mind that whatever the weather conditions are in the moment, there is a way forward. To make progress, it is key to focus on the opportunities that may come to pass in a week, a month, or perhaps in a year or two. There is humility in knowing that you cannot predict the future environment or opportunity to invest and advance.

The next six chapters offer basic tools that are useful in being able to shift strategy and adapt the plan when weather conditions change. Adapting does not mean the team improvises an ascent without making sure the team has the skills to handle it. In climbing and investing, adapting a plan that exceeds the abilities of the team is one of the most frequent mistakes made, and it is costly in terms of time and wasted resources.

Humility is a much-underappreciated tool for success in adverse situations. The most experienced climbers use external resources in times when veering off course is required. They engage fellow experienced climbers, the Sherpas, and their team. So too should CIOs engage the guidance of other experienced CIOs, their external managers, and their teams in adjusting the strategic plan.

6

Portfolio Construction

In climbing, having confidence in your partners is no small concern. One climber's actions can affect the welfare of the entire team. The consequences of a poorly tied knot, a stumble, a dislodged rock, or some other careless deed are as likely to be felt by the perpetrator's colleagues as the perpetrator.
— John Krakauer, *Into Thin Air*[1]

Portfolio construction involves the implementation of the policy portfolio over time. For many experienced alpinists, portfolio construction is truly the art of investing because the process and technique may not guarantee success, but they definitely increase the probability of success. Every decision must be made balancing risk and potential return. The art is being able to think specifically on a single task, while at the next step think broadly to anticipate what may be needed around the next precipice. The mental challenge is to think in two horizons; making sure the expedition survives what is immediately in front, while being open to new ideas that provide an opportunity at some point later in the climb.

The policy portfolio sets the road map, but portfolio construction sets the strategy by which the endowment can optimally deliver both beta and alpha expectations. Table 6.1 provides a list of considerations in constructing an endowment portfolio. Constructing a portfolio with

---

[1] Jon Krakauer, *Into Thin Air* (New York: Knopf Doubleday Publishing Group, 1998).

Table 6.1

Considerations for Portfolio Construction
• Selecting market beta exposure
• Diversification of alpha sources
• Designing strategy within each asset class
• Manager concentration versus diversification
• Sizing of managers
• Reassessing sizing
• Rebalancing ranges
• Internal Process

Source: The William and Flora Hewlett Foundation.

differentiated sources of beta and alpha is key to generating consistently superior returns.

Selecting Market Beta Exposure

As we noted in the chapters on public and private asset classes, there are significant differences in the market exposure a portfolio can have depending on the choices and the objective for each asset class. Return from market beta can be generated in many different ways based on the underlying strategies. Exposure selection can be based on the expected strong return from beta or from a segment of the asset class that is deemed to be a rich alpha source.

This is the point at which it is important to triage which market exposures are interesting and which ones aren't so the team understands where to focus their efforts and efficiently uses their time. In addition, there needs to be current analysis on the depth and size of the subsector market beta being considered to identify if the opportunity is scalable and also to pre-identify whether managers will face challenges executing the strategy as promised.

Deployment into an asset class can be done either from a top-down basis using the policy portfolio as the target weight in the portfolio, or on a bottom-up basis based on the opportunities and individual manager decisions. Most teams figure out the market beta exposure, using both bottom-up manager ideas and the policy portfolio targets.

Diversification of Alpha Sources

The endowment policy portfolio has, as its core belief, that a portfolio benefits from diversification of beta exposure, since not all assets move up or down at the same time. Portfolios can benefit from having diversified sources of alpha. Put another way, the managers selected in each asset class should be expected to generate excess returns in idiosyncratic ways.

Designing Asset Class Strategy

Taking into consideration the role of the asset class within the endowment, each asset class director pursues a strategy aimed at delivering the return and risk expectations that have been set for the following decade. Individually, each asset class has realized active risk resulting from a series of individual fundamentally driven decisions made on a bottom-up basis. Each director is responsible for delivering the beta of the asset class plus alpha within the risk budget assumed in the policy portfolio.

At the asset class level, the CIO and/or asset class director may decide what segments of the asset class offer the best expected return per unit of risk. Understanding the efficiency of the benchmark of the asset class can be useful in identifying areas where active managers can exploit an area of the market that is mismatched to the official benchmark. For example, a real estate strategy may be weighted toward multifamily apartments or logistics and have little exposure to office. The decision can be made in the selection of managers on a bottom-up basis, or on a top-down basis by intentionally hiring managers in the sectors identified by the director as offering the most attractive long-term opportunity.

Philosophy of Concentration versus Diversified Managers

Some investors want to have a concentrated group of managers because they think of the portfolio as a collection of the underlying assets, and therefore with a concentrated manager roster investors can know what they own. Active managers have periods when they do well and times when alpha fails to materialize, so it is good to have a portfolio of at least 10 managers per asset class to generate consistency of alpha.

Concentrating managers creates greater tracking error (active risk) and the possibility of generating higher alpha than a diversified manager approach (20–40 managers in each asset class). The concentrated manager approach is typically adopted by teams that invest in a highly integrated manner, are confident in manager selection, and are incentivized to generate returns on the diversified pool of assets. The concentration of the manager's underlying portfolio needs to be considered to ensure proper diversification of idiosyncratic risk.

At Hewlett, we believe that knowing what we own at the portfolio-company level helps us have confidence in the endowment's ability to generate return and confidence in our managers' ability to execute their strategies. Knowing the underlying portfolio companies and assets requires the CIO and team to roll up their sleeves and assess how the managers and underlying portfolio assets have potential to generate return across the entire portfolio.

Many investment programs are designed to have 80–150 managers to reduce the risk that any single manager will fail to deliver on the execution of the strategy. The flip side is that no single-manager alpha can help deliver portfolio alpha for an asset class, since the impact is muted on both the upside and the downside. In effect, investors who believe in hiring a diversified asset class roster focus more on the performance of the manager, and less on the assets underneath. This philosophy is typically adopted by teams that are incentivized to generate returns within their asset class because having a diversified roster of managers within the asset class improves the probability that the asset class portfolio can achieve the return of the benchmark (the expected beta is earned), plus or minus some amount that will not imperil the career of the asset class director. One final note, depending on the staffing model, having a large number of people working on one or two asset classes may encourage having a larger number of managers in the roster.

Sizing of Managers

The term "sizing of managers" refers to the size of the organization's investment with a manager relative to the NAV of the portfolio. The portfolio benefits from having a framework that adjusts sizing of managers based on risk of the market exposure and also probability of success in execution of the strategy by the manager. Allocators have to consider a double layer of risk: quantitative risks that can be measured through tracking error and volatility, and qualitative risks that are harder to assess. The goal is to de-risk expected return as much as possible. The size of the position should be based on the relationship between the (realistic) expected time-weighted return (TWR) net of fees and the expected risk the manager will take to achieve the return.

You would be unsurprised to find that at Hewlett we take into consideration the difficulty of the climb when choosing our climbing partners. There are excellent managers that are sized modestly in our portfolio simply because we concluded that the difficulty of the strategy was high, even though we have great confidence in their ability to execute and generate alpha. We also tend to not invest in geographies or sectors where we find that the exogenous risks complicate the ability of the manager or the portfolio companies to achieve the strategic objectives. In both instances, the manager quality may be excellent, but the opportunity set limits our sizing.

Sizing manager exposure is a bit more challenging for private investments. The initial commitment must be sized taking into account the expectation of future commitments as the manager raises additional funds. For subsequent fund raises, investors must consider the NAV already invested with the manager, potential distributions back to LPs, and the pace at which the manager is expected to invest new capital commitments. Each private asset class has slightly different pacing in fund-raising and investment periods; as such the asset class strategy should model the exposure of the existing manager roster looking forward 5–10 years.

When we discuss a new private investment manager for the Hewlett portfolio, we assume we are making a decision for three fund cycles. While at every fund cycle we retain the right to not make a new commitment, when the GP raises the subsequent (second) fund, there is little information on the current fund being underwritten. By the time the GP raises the fund after that (third fund), the LP has enough information from investments in the first fund to assess portfolio construction and diligence. However, the second fund is being invested, and there are unlikely to be more than one or two events that show progress on value creation and perhaps a few distributions of capital back to LPs. As such, underwriting the third fund offers only slightly more information than the current fund under consideration.

Reassessing Sizing

The expected return for a manager should be reviewed on a regular basis. While looking at past, and especially recent, performance is useful, that is in the past. The goal is to resize based on expected return and the expected risk going forward. This process requires reassessing both quantitative and qualitative factors.

A useful tool in assessing whether changes need to be made to portfolio construction within each asset class is monitoring the consistency of alpha over a rolling three-year period and the correlation of alpha to the underlying beta. In addition, investors can then analyze whether the return generated by the manager compensated the portfolio for the active risk taken by the manager. At this point, the asset class director also needs to assess whether the manager took more risk than was underwritten. At the qualitative level, the asset class director must also understand if there are changes in the manager's firm or life that could be a potential headwind to continued generation of alpha going forward.

After all, the ability to generate return at the endowment level is a result of the individual decisions made on a manager-by-manager basis. Getting the size decision right is important because the return generated by each manager times the size of the manager is what contributes to portfolio return. Being right on the manager decision counts, but investors need to have sized the position large enough for it to matter to the portfolio.

Sizing often needs to be reconsidered based on the needs of the endowment for cash flow. In any given year, roughly 10–15% of an institutional portfolio turns over due to capital calls, distributions, new investment opportunities, redeeming managers, payout, and so on. While the endowment has a long-term horizon, the reality is that successful investors make decisions taking the needs of the endowment into account that do not necessarily have anything to do with the quality or conviction of a manager or strategy. Having a framework for evaluating sizing decisions allows the portfolio to adapt to changing conditions.

Rebalancing Ranges

The term "rebalancing" refers to the adjustment in the weights of different asset classes. Core to rebalancing is the concept that markets and asset classes mean-revert over time to a "normal" risk premium. If an asset class returns higher-than-normal risk premiums for a time period, investors should expect the asset class to under-earn the normal risk premium in the subsequent period. Rebalancing is recommended in order to maintain the deployment of the portfolio in line with the policy portfolio. Typically, investors decide to rebalance portfolios when the change in weighting relative to the policy weight exceeds a certain amount. The agreed-upon amount by which the actual portfolio weight in an asset class is allowed to differ on either the upside or downside of the policy target weight is referred to as the rebalancing range.

The evolution of broadly diversified portfolios has introduced limitations to the applicability of rebalancing. There are various considerations in the design of rebalancing ranges. First, investors should consider the deviation from the policy weight that would prompt a rebalancing event. Investors should also consider whether ranges will be applied to specific asset classes or groups of asset classes with high correlations. Finally, there should be agreement with the IC on whether rebalancing actions are mandated or simply serve as a nudge to reevaluate capital deployment.

In practice, investors should consider cost, impact to portfolio construction and manager relationships, and ability to implement rebalancing given illiquid fund structures or lock-up restrictions. Rebalancing ranges are most useful when designed to provide flexibility to the investment team to pursue the long-term strategy of the portfolio. In addition, the greater the weighting of private assets in the portfolio, the more limited is the ability to rebalance the remaining assets. For this reason, it may prove useful to not set rebalancing ranges either too granularly (at the asset class level) or too tightly.

During the 2003–2007 period when Hewlett was building the diversified portfolio, the IC reviewed the deployment of the portfolio against the agreed-upon rebalancing ranges. Over time, the rebalancing ranges were adapted to the risk framework that we use to manage the endowment. Once the portfolio exceeded 30% private investments, portfolio rebalancing was limited as a capital allocation tool. We combined asset classes into groups and aggregated the policy exposures for the group. We set rebalancing ranges as guardrails we use to think about risk and deployment of capital. Given the significant deployment in private asset classes, the IC acknowledged that at times portfolio deployment could fall outside the agreed-upon range. As such, the Hewlett IC does not require immediate action to correct the imbalance created by factors beyond the team's control.

Internal Process

Portfolio risk is something that all investors need to be aware of at every decision point. Investing is a profession that requires sound judgment and experience managing portfolios during varying economic regimes. Protecting against the internal biases can be most effectively managed by establishing a clear process and ensuring that every member of the team is adhering to the process by contributing high-quality work. The range of possible outcomes is wide, and as investors we control only a part of what drives investment returns.

One of the critical biases nearly all investors have is waking up believing that they can beat the market odds. Optimism is inherent in the psychology of investing. The job is to protect against the hubris this can create. Another common blind spot is believing that a decision is rational because it can be justified by data and numbers. Backward-looking data can lead to confidence even though we acknowledge that realized returns or data doesn't predict future results.

Creating a framework for active discussion about the potential range of outcomes often generates insights that move the team forward and protect against complacency. A top-level risk framework categorizes portfolio risk into two groups: internal portfolio risks, over which investors have some level of control, and exogenous risks that are outside investors' control.

At Hewlett, managing internal portfolio risk involves four levels:

1. The process starts with due diligence of a new or existing manager. The objective of the due diligence process is to underwrite how an investment manager creates value over time and the firm's philosophy of people and process. Once the assessment of the manager has concluded, then we assess how the strategy and manager fit into the portfolio. The investment case includes a discussion of potential return and risks, including exogenous event risks that could impact the risk-reward framework.

2. Once the investment is part of the portfolio, the investment team is tasked with evaluating whether each manager is executing the strategy as underwritten. Typically, this process occurs when a private manager is raising a subsequent fund and a decision needs to be made about whether to make a commitment to the firm's new fund vehicle. Unfortunately, there isn't a similar forcing mechanism that naturally creates the impetus for underwriting existing investments in public asset classes. Creating an internal process for periodic review and due diligence of every public market investment allows the team to make a fresh assessment of the firm and strategy, and provides the younger members of the investment team the opportunity to understand the rationale for decisions made long ago in public asset classes.

3. A third level comes through the work of the asset class team conducting annual deep dives into the strategy, portfolio construction, and contribution of the asset class to the overall portfolio.

4. Finally, we have a framework that fosters balance between positioning the portfolio for future opportunity and risk-centric awareness. This could take the form of a detailed attribution system, or a deeper understanding of how efficient the investment team has been in generating excess return per unit of risk.

Exogenous Risks

Investors have always managed to make decisions in the face of incomplete information and uncertainty in financial markets. While investors accept this uncertainty, there are times when exogenous risks are more prominent in surfacing a wider range of outcomes than at other times. Very few institutional investors have any edge in analyzing exogenous factors. Instead, investors can analyze the impact of these exogenous events on their portfolios through scenario modeling and modeling of portfolio volatility, using stressed correlations. Understanding exogenous risks also helps with manager engagement and portfolio construction.

One of the advantages in managing an institutional portfolio is being able to ignore short-term noise and remain focused on the long term. Nevertheless, the investment team, the board, and the IC are likely to ask for input from the CIO on current market conditions. I have found it useful to have a four-part framework for discussing exogenous factors with the IC and board, that is, a framework that clearly identifies the risk, potential catalyst, expected probability of the event occurring, and potential impact on the portfolio.

Importantly, having a framework should not lead to overconfidence that investors have any control over when or if exogenous events occur. However, there is some comfort in being prepared for the potential impact of an exogenous event and ensuring that the expedition team can survive and the investment objective can still be achieved. Being prepared allows room for courage, and it takes courage to use moments of uncertainty as opportunities to lean in.

The art of portfolio construction and portfolio management is knowing how to shift beta exposures and alpha opportunities over time. The lens through which a CIO views exposures shifts depending on the prominent factors impacting markets. It is sensible to think about exposure in terms of equity risk and non-equity-risk buckets. Other times, it makes sense to think in terms of private and public buckets. The asset allocation model provides long-term guideposts, but with years of experience a CIO should be able to intuitively know if the portfolio is exhibiting higher correlation among private assets than is modeled simply because leverage and liquidity are more prominent factors impacting markets.

The advantage of managing a portfolio with 36 years of experience is the ability to recognize when the results of a model are not representing actual portfolio risk. There are times when the portfolio may be "running hot," not because the risk model says it is, but because I can see the underlying holdings in the portfolio and get a sense of how many of our managers are leaning into risk. There are times when I have to check to see if we have enough risk in the portfolio, and if we don't, adjust sizing of an allocation with one or a few managers. Combining intuition and data is at the core of portfolio management. The next several chapters address different techniques to help the expedition team overcome challenges or make opportunistic progress.

7

Active Risk

The art of mountaineering is knowing when to go, when to stay, and when to retreat.

—Ed Viesturs[1]

"Active risk" is defined as the volatility of excess returns, and is sometimes referred to as tracking error from the benchmark. Taking active risk is necessary to generate portfolio alpha; otherwise the return of the portfolio would be equal to the benchmark return less management fees. It is by generating excess return (alpha) that a portfolio can shift the risk-adjusted return above the optimized policy portfolio expected return. However, the flexibility in constructing the portfolio to generate alpha has the potential to introduce additional excess return not captured in the asset allocation study. There are active risks inherent in portfolio construction and implementation that include but are not limited to the list on Table 7.1.

Measuring Active Risk

Active risk is how investors can measure portfolio construction skills. Climbers look for clues along the path such as rappel anchors or flags

---

[1] Ed Viesturs and David Roberts, *No Shortcuts to the Top: Climbing the World's 14 Highest Peaks* (New York: Crown, 2007).

Table 7.1

Active Risk Considerations
• Manager selection
• Concentrated manager roster
• Style biases
• Strategy tilts
• Geographic tilts
• Deployment versus policy tilts

Source: The William and Flora Hewlett Foundation.

to know they are on the right path. Realized active risk is an important clue that can be calculated at the asset class and the aggregate portfolio level. The realized excess return earned above the benchmark (alpha) can also be observed. In effect, the return from active risk is the return earned by the portfolio in the implementation of the policy asset mix.

In practice, understanding whether the portfolio was compensated for additional units of risk is called the information ratio. The information ratio is simply the realized annualized alpha divided by the realized active risk. The team can then analyze the information ratio and test the potential of additional sources of active risk. For robust calculations, it is best to use a five-year rolling data set.

The same diversification benefit gained in asset allocation when investors combine different market beta exposures (asset classes) exists when investors combine different sources of alpha (returns in excess of the benchmark). As such, even if each asset class portfolio has a realized active risk/tracking error of 4–6%, when the diversified alpha sources are combined, the active risk at the aggregate portfolio level is much lower, typically 2–3%. A successful investment team aims to deliver a long-term information ratio of 0.50–0.75 or 100–200 bps above the benchmark (alpha).

Investors may want to consider the correlation between the beta return and the alpha to arrive at the contribution to portfolio risk from active risk. A simple framework begins with calculating realized active risk of each asset class and the realized correlation for a 10-year period. Ideally, the investment team is able to consistently generate alpha with zero or negative correlation to the return from market beta. The impact of the active risk resulting from the various factors noted in Table 7.1 can then be considered against the realized volatility of the policy portfolio benchmark.

Realized active risk within an asset class can be defined as the tracking error of the realized return of the asset class when compared to the asset class benchmark. Concentrated manager portfolios tend to have realized active risk between 4% and 6%. Broadly diversified manager rosters within an asset class tend to have realized active risk between 1% and 3% as each additional manager added to the portfolio diversifies the impact of idiosyncratic risk from any individual manager.

It is fair to analyze the information ratio within each asset class to understand if changes in portfolio construction are warranted. If most asset classes are generating information ratios of 0.5–0.8, then one can conclude the investment team has been efficient in generating excess return per unit of risk. In examining longer time periods, it is important to acknowledge that private asset classes sometimes suffer multi-year dry spells.

Size Limitations to Active Risk

The challenge of constructing portfolios with enough active risk to have an opportunity to generate alpha is greater for large pools of capital. For investment teams managing smaller pools of assets that allow access to managers with idiosyncratic strategies and employ some or all of the tools for creating active risk mentioned in the bullet points, constructing a portfolio with active risk of 2–3% is possible. Thus, the endowment has the possibility of earning 100–150 basis points of annualized alpha if the team is successful in generating an information ratio of 0.5.

However, very large pools of capital, such as sovereign wealth funds or pension plans, have constraints in the ability to construct asset class portfolios with active risk greater than 2%. They may not have access to the same manager roster or be constrained in their ability to employ strategic tilts. When aggregated together, the aggregate active risk of very large pools of capital is typically 0.75–1.25%. Again, assuming the team is successful in generating an information ratio of 0.5, this means the large pool of assets has the possibility of earning only 38–75 basis points of annualized alpha. Of course, for sovereign wealth funds and pension funds the absolute dollars of contribution to return from alpha is worth the effort of assembling a large investment team.

It is tempting to think that increasing active risk could always result in greater excess-return generation. In thinking through the implications of increasing active risk in each asset class, it becomes clear that there are limitations in a team's ability to do so, regardless of size. Increasing active risk can be done primarily in public markets, and the goal is to build a portfolio that can survive a downturn without capitulation.

Setting Expectations of Annualized Alpha

How the investment team is incentivized to generate return is likely to have an impact on how the team constructs the portfolio and the appetite for taking active risk. If the organization measures the success of an asset class director primarily on the return of their asset class, then the director is likely to design an asset class strategy that ensures he/she will be able to consistently deliver the return from the market beta plus a bit of alpha. Typically, this takes the form of an asset class portfolio investing across 20–40 managers resulting in low active risk, and limited opportunity to generate alpha. In effect, the asset class holdings are broadly diversified and represent the index. There are several reasons this happens; the two most often heard are: (1) the asset class director is managing career risk and doesn't want to take too much active risk and underperform the benchmark, and (2) the asset class director is starting out and has yet to develop confidence in manager-selection skills and hires a variety of managers to be safe.

In contrast, if an investment team is incentivized to generate alpha at the aggregate portfolio level, instead of the asset class level, the asset class director is more likely to design an asset class portfolio with enough active risk to have a high probability of generating sufficient alpha at the asset class level so that it makes a meaningful contribution to aggregate portfolio alpha. There is one reason that this happens; namely, in any five-year period, each asset class is likely to underperform the benchmark, yet the asset class director knows he/she will not be penalized because the incentive is generated at the aggregate portfolio level.

It helps to manage expectations with the IC and the team if there is a framework to set expectations for alpha generation at the asset class and portfolio level. An investment team that has an observable information ratio of 0.5, and actively uses many of the portfolio-construction tools noted in the bullet points at the beginning of this chapter, is likely to implement the policy portfolio with 2–3% tracking error/active risk. It would be fair to set an expectation of alpha contribution to return of the aggregate endowment of 100–150 basis points per annum.

Employing a similar methodology by asset class, one can observe the realized information ratio over the past 5–10 years. If the asset class director and asset class strategy have remained largely unchanged, then it is fair to set an expectation of alpha for the coming decade based on what the asset class has been able to contribute to overall portfolio alpha. In sum, each director is responsible for delivering the return from the market beta of the asset class plus alpha (excess return above the asset class benchmark).

8

Portfolio Hedging

A sudden ripping sound a thousand feet above makes us look up. Out of nowhere appear a pair of whirlwinds. Caused by the straining of wind through the turrets of the pillar, they tear at the ice and rock, scouring and feeding on the mountain like a living organism. They reach a frenetic pitch, then subside as suddenly as they appeared, dropping lumps of ice tinkling down the walls.

—Greg Child, *Thin Air*[1]

C louds in the investment horizon appear out of nowhere, and suddenly it can snow. Over the years, successful investors learn to remain unemotional during periods of market stress and take shelter in the crevices to wait out the storm. One way to build resiliency into an investment program is to diversify market exposure by investing in several asset classes, and portfolio construction. Hedging is another way investors build resilience into investment portfolios by reducing short-term volatility to weather the storm.

The classic definition of hedging is protecting an asset against losses using options or futures. By focusing on the desired objective – short-term volatility management or alpha generation – it is easier to have a conversation about the benefits and drawbacks of implementing a

---

[1] Greg Child, *Thin Air: Encounters in the Himalayas* (Seattle: Mountaineers Books), Chapter 3.

hedging strategy. As we noted in Chapter 1 on setting objectives of the investment program, for some stakeholders adopting a hedging program to improve the probability that the portfolio is able to generate returns on a consistent basis may be worth the cost and effort of employing a hedging program.

As with so many decisions made by the investment team, the reason to hedge is highly correlated with the risk appetite and liquidity needs of the institution. Of the three primary risks of an investment portfolio (volatility, illiquidity, and drawdown), hedging programs aim to address volatility and drawdown risk. The risks can be managed by implementing active hedging or volatility management strategies.

Being realistic about the skills Hewlett needed to manage a hedging strategy was a key consideration related to portfolio hedging. The Hewlett investment team is focused on portfolio construction and manager selection, not on macroeconomic trends and market timing. In the end, we reasoned that the time allocation of the team and the complexity of a hedging program would not be additive to long-term endowment returns.

A CIO could deem it prudent to engage in a hedge option strategy to return the portfolio to the policy risk level instead of actively shifting allocations with existing managers. This is particularly the case when assets are illiquid and cannot be added or redeemed in a cost-effective or timely manner. This may also occur when there is limited capacity with a GP and redemptions forego the ability to have future capacity with the manager. Some investors adopt risk-hedging strategies because they are relatively new to the investment program, and believe the organization would be unable to withstand the shock of loss. The most common risks institutional portfolios might hedge are listed in Table 8.1.

In an ideal world, investors would be able to minimize volatility risk and be able to maintain consistent funding budgets. Unfortunately, there is a certain level of risk that any investor and organization must

Table 8.1

Common Risks to Potentially Hedge
• Volatility risk
• Equity market loss
• Inflation
• Interest rate increases
• Single-stock risk

Source: The William and Flora Hewlett Foundation.

assume in order to achieve a return objective sufficiently high to fund the needs of an institution. The balance between return and risk is the tension between impairment of the long-term purchasing power of the organization against the risk of portfolio drawdown.

Hedging strategies are fundamentally rooted in the belief that past correlations, whether positive or negative, will occur in the future. It is difficult, however, to have great confidence in correlation models since much of what capital markets have experienced in the past 15 years has been the result of extraordinary and new monetary and fiscal policies. There isn't precedent to model out with a high degree of certainty how the unraveling of these stimulus measures could impact correlations.

Active Hedging Strategy

Active hedging strategies aim to reduce the estimated volatility of portfolios as a structural part of the investment strategy. Active hedging requires macro skills, trading skills, behavioral psychology, and a lot of humility. The highest probability of capturing the desired return of a hedge comes from actively managing a program to adapt the composition of the hedge over the life of the hedge. It sounds complex, and it is. To complicate matters even further, how a hedge actually performs under stressed market conditions cannot be fully predicted. This makes it challenging to accurately predict the ultimate payoff and degree to which the portfolio is protected on an ex-ante basis.

Pricing of hedging strategies is variable, and the length of the holding period without suffering an adverse event in the portfolio significantly impacts the analysis of cost versus reward of the hedge. There is a negative expected return from hedging. For some institutions, it may be that premiums paid for insurance are well-spent, even if the intent is to never have the coverage triggered.

Identifying Risks to Hedge

Determining the type of hedging instrument to use depends on the clear identification of the risk investors want to hedge out. It sounds obvious, yet many investors who fail to clearly define the source of risk they want to manage often find hedges didn't work as they had imagined.

Expected volatility risk is probably the risk most institutional investors worry about since boards and ICs tend to observe returns over short time periods despite being long-term investors. In theory, the policy portfolio expected volatility serves as the midpoint of a symmetric band around which portfolio risk may find itself, given moves in capital markets. In practice, there are times when expected portfolio risk runs above or below the policy risk target and bands. The most common reason why expected portfolio volatility runs well above or below the bands is due to a material up/down move in an asset class.

Protecting against equity market loss typically includes options such as puts on the S&P 500 Index or NASDAQ, volatility instruments such as VIX[2], and/or equity market shorts on the index obtained via swap instruments. When investors hedge by buying equity market puts, the loss to the portfolio is limited to the premium paid for the put and the extent to which the put level differed from the strike price. Puts allow the portfolio to retain full upside capture.

Protecting against inflation is more complex. It helps to determine if the portfolio benefits from protection against the change in the level of inflation or change in inflation expectations (i.e., the volatility in expected inflation). Depending on whether the objective is protection against change in level or expectations, the hedging tools available are inflation swaps, TIPS, and linkers.[3] Possible hedges include gold, hiring a CTA[4] to capture commodity price rises, or purchasing currency swaps to capture inflation differentials between countries.

Protecting against interest rate increases also requires identifying the exact cause of the rate increase to be identified before constructing a hedge. If the portfolio is deemed to be over-exposed to credit risk, then it may make sense to buy credit default swaps as protection. Concern over the slope of the yield curve requires a very different set of hedges.

Protecting against single-stock risk is typically undertaken by institutions diversifying away from significant equity ownership in a publicly listed company by the donor or family office. The board can approve a plan to have the CIO engage an investment bank to create a systematic program for selling down the single-stock position over time. The organization needs to consider the extent to which the single-stock exposure

---

[2] VIX is the Chicago Board Options Exchange Volatility Index, which measures 30-day expected volatility of the U.S. equity market using the price of call and put options.

[3] TIPS are inflation-indexed securities issued by the U.S. Treasury. Linkers refer to inflation-linked securities issued by the governments of UK, Australia, Canada, Mexico, and Sweden. As of February 2022, there were $4.4 trillion inflation-linked bonds outstanding.

[4] CTAs are commodity trading advisors.

increases the volatility of the portfolio, as well as any implications on voting rights associated with reducing exposure over time. Other organizations restrict investing in the industry related to the single stock to improve diversification. In rare cases, when the legal team has cleared it, the investment office can hedge the single-stock position using put options on the security.

Hedge Ratio

Once the risk has been identified, the team must decide how much of the market exposure in the portfolio should be hedged. Presumably, some exposure to market beta is desired, or else it should have been excluded in the design of the policy portfolio. The hedge ratio refers to the value of the hedge open position relative to the underlying market exposure in the portfolio. For example, a portfolio has $100 million invested with an active manager in a market that the team wants to maintain, but wants to protect potential downside. The team wants only $50 million of exposure to the equity market and decides to hedge the other $50 million for a hedge ratio of 0.5. The hedge ratio matters because this, and the cost of hedging (premium), determine the efficiency of the hedging program.

Time Horizon

An institution that stands to benefit from a long-term structural hedging program is best served by hiring an expert in creating a diversified book of hedging instruments. There are institutions that create structural hedging programs that allow the portfolio to deploy a higher level of equity risk and earn a higher expected return (net of hedging costs), with the same drawdown profile.

Tactical hedging strategies where investors attempt to "market-time" by adding or removing hedges are very difficult since they require macro skills and trading skills. In some cases, the investment team may have the skills to structure and manage a hedging program internally. However, the staffing cost and operational challenges need to be considered against the alternative of hiring an external hedge manager.

Institutional Tolerance for Volatility

For some institutions, inability to fully capture the upside of equity markets during years of positive market returns would impair their ability to grow the endowment long term to fund a broad array of projects desired by the board. For other institutions, giving up 100 basis points of return every year in a hedging program would dampen returns to the point where payout could be impaired.

There are institutional investors that have asset-liability matching obligations for whom a structural hedging program is a prudent idea. There are also wealth management firms for whom delivering consistent returns to their clients is an existential activity. The tolerance for changes in asset value over a three-year period may differ across the client base; therefore spending 100 basis points per year of return on hedging makes sense for an organization to thrive and retain clients.

In contrast, there are institutions that have a long-term horizon and capacity to absorb significant losses because their spending needs remain low, or there is a plan for material capital injections into the endowment. These types of institutions do not typically hedge exposure because they have liquidity and the patience to hold the assets in the portfolio through the downturn without any need to liquidate at "drawdown" levels.

At Hewlett, we balance growth of the endowment with the desire to generate consistent returns, given that we fund 100% of the activities of the foundation. We considered whether our granting activity could withstand a drawdown scenario of a temporary loss of value of 20%. While hedging to reduce the severity of a downside correction in the value of the endowment is similar to buying an insurance policy, we felt the reduction in the long-term expected return of the portfolio by the annual cost of the hedge book was not in the best interest of the endowment. Instead, working with the president and board we developed a mix of alternatives to having a structural hedging program.

Volatility Management Strategy

The objective of volatility management is similar to having rebalancing ranges for the policy portfolio. Volatility management is a tool for selectively hedging to manage deployment to public asset classes when exposures are dictated by the capital markets or the actions of our underlying managers. It is done on exception-only to solve a temporary issue.

In theory, the policy risk target should serve as the midpoint of a symmetric band around which actual portfolio risk may find itself, given capital market moves.[5] In practice, however, there are times when portfolio risk runs above/below the policy risk target and above/below the bands. There are two instances why, on a qualitative or quantitative basis, the CIO would deem it prudent to engage in using derivative exposure to return portfolio risk to the agreed-upon policy risk level at the portfolio level and within a single asset class.

At the Portfolio Level

Volatility risk management is most useful when the exposure of an asset class moves materially, either due to a significant rally or correction, resulting in a material move in the volatility risk of the portfolio. If the asset class exposure is well above policy target, there are hedging tools to manage risk while remaining committed to a three-year rolling commitment budget, and maintaining hard-won capacity at private managers, without engaging in a secondary sale or selling public equities to solve a temporary issue. A hedge is preferred to redeeming the position when assets are (a) illiquid and cannot be bought or sold in a cost-effective manner or (b) capital cannot be easily added or withdrawn due to capacity constraints.

It is difficult to draw stark lines between managing volatility at the portfolio and asset class level, given the reflexivity of risk across the portfolio. In the same vein, if the public equity market declines significantly, and the public equity asset class shrinks well below policy target, the CIO could use derivatives to rebuild public equity exposure as managers open capacity over time. The flexibility to do so is a practical tool for generating consistent risk-adjusted return.

Within an Asset Class

There are periods of time when the underlying portfolio within an asset class may exhibit higher beta (market risk exposure) than what was allocated in the risk model. On these occasions the CIO is faced with the decision of giving up capacity in managers that consistently generate alpha in order to solve what is likely a temporary issue or employ derivative strategies for volatility risk management.

---

[5] In practice, an institution could have negative asymmetry in the bands since it is natural to have a greater aversion to unanticipated loss resulting from running the portfolio above estimated policy risk than the acceptance of having foregone upside in the markets by running the portfolio below estimated portfolio risk.

In September 2017, Hewlett hired a manager to implement a put protection program to manage the volatility risk of the public equity asset class. Despite being at target policy exposure, the beta (market exposure) of the public equity portfolio was at a 16% premium to the long-term average and a 35% premium to the three-year average as several of our managers that consistently generate alpha individually rotated into growth stocks. Roughly 85% of the increase in beta was attributable to five managers that had consistently contributed the highest amount of alpha. These same public equity managers had been closed to additional capital, and we were reluctant to give up Hewlett's capacity to address what we believed to be a temporary issue. The most effective way to manage the increased contribution of the public equity asset class to the overall volatility of the endowment was to buy puts on the S&P 500 Index. When the individual managers shifted the exposure and the beta of the public equity portfolio reverted to long-term average, the derivative program was terminated.

Alternatives to Hedging

Clearly stating the negative event investors desire to hedge helps to creatively think of ways to address the issue. Together, the CIO, the organization's president, and the board have the opportunity to collaborate to provide flexibility to the investment program. In doing so, having alternative solutions greatly improves the resilience of the investment program and the organization.

Credit lines: To provide the institution with the time necessary to recover the value of the assets in the portfolio, it needs to be able to fund spending and obligations (net capital calls) from sources external to the portfolio. Securing lines of credit to provide flexibility is an alternative to hedging without the structural drag on returns. If the organization has sufficient liquidity to fund operations, either with cash or using the institution's credit line, then the investment program is likely to be able to withstand a temporary loss of value without being forced to crystallize losses by selling assets at "distressed" prices.

Flexibility in spending: Working alongside the organization, there may be a way to design spending needs to adjust downward after a predetermined negative event in capital markets. Endowments have the benefit of multiple sources of income to fund the operations of the university.

Family offices may or may not have flexibility depending on the needs of family members; however, adapting spending could be a good option.

Adopting a new policy portfolio: Despite best intentions to determine the risk tolerance of the IC and board, there are times when the reality of potential loss becomes too great for the IC and board to contemplate. If there is a view that the portfolio's expected risk is above the tolerance of the organization, then adopting a new asset allocation policy that decreases equity market risk is preferable to bearing the cost and risk of hedging.

At Hewlett, the president and board adopted a flexible spending model that adjusts spending downward during times of market stress. Having agreed to the long-term policy risk level, the IC and board understand that in order to benefit from the growth in public and private equities there will be years of mark-to-market losses. They agreed that managing equity market risk through portfolio construction is preferable to the cost of hedging. In Hewlett's case, the credit lines and flexible spend model provide sufficient breathing room to manage the investment program through a crisis without the use of traditional hedging strategies. In addition, volatility management provides the investment team with the tools to manage during challenging periods. We agreed that if in the future the IC and board determine that the estimated portfolio risk is above the tolerance of the institution, then we would adopt a new asset allocation that decreases equity market risk, instead of bearing the cost and risk of hedging.

9

Liquidity Management

A man's accomplishments in life are the cumulative effect of his attention to detail.

—John Foster Dulles[1]

L iquidity management is the practice of figuring out the plan each year to secure sufficient liquidity to fund payout, net capital calls, and new investment opportunities. Amidst all of the challenges and joys that come with managing the portfolio, selecting managers, and managing the team, there is no more important function for a successful investor than ensuring there is sufficient liquidity to meet the needs of the organization. Successful investment teams manage liquidity with a view to balancing the priority of retaining flexibility during stress periods, against the opportunity cost of maximizing illiquidity premium earned.

There is no specific level of illiquid investments that is appropriate across institutional portfolios with a long-term investment horizon. The definition of illiquid assets includes investments in fund structures, typically 10 years in duration, in venture, buyout, real estate, infrastructure, and natural resources. It also includes public investments in share classes

---

[1] Leonard Mosley, *Dulles: A Biography of Eleanor, Allen, and John Foster Dulles and Their Family Network* (New York: Doubleday, 1978).

where investors cannot redeem capital for three years, as well as 10-year fund structures in public asset classes.

The deployment of the portfolio across illiquid assets is not entirely in the control of the investment team since significant market moves can move the deployment of the portfolio away from the policy portfolio agreed upon with the IC. The CIO must manage the liquidity of the portfolio without having the ability to shift allocation, since there are limited options to shift the allocation to private assets once made.

Illiquidity Tolerance

Tolerance for illiquidity differs between normal market cycles (base case) and periods when the endowment suffers through significant market corrections (stress case). The probability of a 20%+ drawdown in a single year is low, as large drawdowns are rare events, so the investment team typically spends most of the time operating in an environment consistent with the policy portfolio base case annualized returns.

As we showed in Chapter 5, the probability that a large drawdown will occur at some point over a decade-long period is much higher than most investors and committees expect. Investors should manage the portfolio's liquidity to ensure that, during such a stress case, the organization can meet its legal obligations and minimize the chance that the portfolio must realize losses to maintain a prudently managed portfolio for the long term.

There is a degree of judgment surrounding the point at which institutional portfolios should limit illiquidity during normal times. Advocates for large illiquid exposure would point to the limited capital needs in a single year (payout plus net capital calls) and believe the additional expected return from illiquid asset classes is worth the risk of distorting portfolio allocations during stressed times. More cautious investors would say that illiquidity risk must be managed to ensure that the institution can survive a stress-case scenario without significantly distorting diversification or exceeding the risk tolerance agreed upon with the IC and board. In addition, the loss of flexibility could impair the portfolio's long-term plan to maintain a three-year rolling commitment budget deemed to be important to maintain the quality of relationships with managers developed over the years.

Table 9.1

Considerations for Managing Portfolio Liquidity
• Securing lines of credit to cover one year of spending
• Cash reserves to take advantage of market dislocations
• Minimizing the institution's use of multi-year spending commitments
• Flexibility in annual spending budget

Source: The William and Flora Hewlett Foundation.

In Table 9.1 are a few areas where an organization can make changes to improve tolerance for illiquidity in the investment program.

Every institution has different spending rules and risk tolerance that guide the appropriate level of portfolio risk and illiquidity risk. The approach to liquidity management and the metrics used to manage portfolios and communicate with the IC vary widely. In general, most institutions track two types of liquidity metrics: coverage of annual spending plus capital calls and positioning ratios, shown in Table 9.2.

Liquidity coverage ratios depend on the cash flow profile of the portfolio and the stage of development of the private asset classes within the diversified portfolio. Organizations with predictable inflows typically look to have one year of spending plus one-third of unfunded commitments available in investments with one year of liquidity or less. Some institutions building private portfolios gain comfort by having liquidity available within six months be equal to or greater than two years of expected payout and capital calls.

Table 9.2

Metrics	Definition	Desired level	Peer ratios
Short-term coverage	$\dfrac{\text{Liquid within 1 year}}{\text{1-year spending + 1-year calls}}$	>2.0	4.2
Medium-term coverage	$\dfrac{\text{Liquid within 2 years}}{\text{2-year spending + 2-year calls}}$	>3.0	4.9
Positioning unfunded/portfolio	$\dfrac{\text{Total unfunded}}{\text{Total portfolio value}}$	16–20%	22%

Source: The William and Flora Hewlett Foundation, July 2019.

Unfunded Commitments

Managing the level of unfunded commitments differs based on whether the objective is to grow the private investment component of the portfolio, or whether the goal is simply to maintain exposure in private asset classes near or at policy portfolio target weight. Managing the forward commitment budget involves having a view on the pace of capital calls and distributions, as well as the relative outperformance of each private asset class relative to the overall portfolio.

During a stress scenario, there will be trade-offs regardless of the level of illiquidity. Paradoxically, reducing the pace of commitments to private asset classes has limited impact on the asset class weights in the subsequent three to five years. This is particularly true in venture since the return profile of the asset class would suggest unfunded commitments to be small relative to the capital already invested. In fact, while cash flow models have limitations, the sensitivity in the output from the models lies almost entirely in the behavior of distributions from the portfolio, and not in the pace of commitments.

That said, there needs to be guidance to the investment team as to the appropriate pace of new commitments to private funds because over a decade, the pace at which the investment portfolio commits to illiquid funds will impact flexibility in managing the portfolio. The starting point of illiquid investments is key in ensuring a degree of flexibility if and when a downward spiral in financial markets shifts deployment and risk.

At the end of 2008, Hewlett's illiquid assets had moved above the optimal level due to the decline in public equity and credit markets. In 2009, a new policy portfolio was designed to reduce the probability that the foundation would be forced to sell assets into difficult markets. We introduced into the portfolio shorter-duration illiquid structures available in distressed credit. By allocating 5–10% of the endowment in shorter-duration illiquid structures, we retained flexibility to pivot toward asset classes where the illiquidity premium was rich. In this way, we diversified exposure across different asset classes and investment horizons to capture diversified sources of illiquidity premium.

On a practical level, investors should take a measured approach to making commitments to private funds so that they have room to maintain the pace of commitments unchanged during challenging periods. A review of the past 20 years of returns by vintage year across the four major private asset classes shows that returns are superior for funds raised and invested in years when funding conditions for the asset class were difficult. Unsurprisingly, poor returns have been consistent in years where the asset class had the benefit of accommodating liquidity conditions and investors demanded little illiquidity premium.

Modeling Portfolio Cash Flows

Many institutions develop cash flow models to manage commitments to private investments and to forecast cash flows for the organization. Table 9.3 lists a few metrics to consider over a three-year time frame that are helpful in communicating across the investment team and with the IC.

Institutions with mature private portfolios have rules of thumb on the pace of calls and distributions. Typically, forecasting calls in any given year is possible with some degree of variability. However, distributions from the existing private portfolio remain unpredictable from one year to the next even in the best constructed private portfolios; therefore, net cash flows are highly variable.

Rules of thumb in private asset class cash flow models tend to be of greater applicability for diversified private GP rosters where the behavior of the aggregate group of GPs is similar to the historical norms used to define the rules of thumb. Cash flow models typically assume that 25% of all outstanding unfunded commitments will be called in a calendar year and 20% of NAV in each private asset class will be distributed in a calendar year.

When private investments are made directly, or through single-asset continuation vehicles, the idiosyncratic nature of each investment will make modeling cash flows more challenging. An investment program that has strategically chosen to have a concentrated roster of managers (15 or fewer) in each private asset class is likely to have more

Table 9.3

Metrics for Modeling Cash Flows
• Expected distributions
• Expected capital calls
• Peak exposure
• Pacing of commitments

Source: The William and Flora Hewlett Foundation.

idiosyncratic behavior in the cash flow model than an organization with a broadly diversified group of managers in each asset class.

Institutions with a concentrated manager roster or with direct investments have the ability to gather real-time information directly from the GP on the investment pace, calls, and potential distributions. Once aggregated, the bottom-up inputs into the cash flow model may serve to identify episodic events and flows and reduce the element of surprise when compared to using the top-down rules-of-thumb model.

In terms of modeling the amount invested in a manager or asset class's "peak exposure" there needs to be careful attention to how the institution intends to scale future commitments (sizing), whether the pace of the commitments to future funds will be faster than the model-implied three to four years (frequency). Lastly, the return assumption used for the asset class or manager on a net of fees basis and the number of years assets are held will also impact the ultimate exposure of the asset class or manager.

A review of the brief 25+-year history of private fund distributions shows that even during "normal times" there are periods when distributions slow significantly. A two-to-three-year dry spell in net distributions from private investments inevitably results in distortions in policy weights across the endowment, as payout is funded from cash, bonds, and hedge funds, while risk is managed down to appropriate levels by selling public equities.

While no model is perfect, cash flow models are useful in checking sizing decisions. They serve the role of having a safety rope in preventing accidental falls. The model also serves as the base for engaging in conversations around the level of exposure that would feel uncomfortably low or high relative to the endowment.

10

Secondaries

You can't go back and change the beginning, but you can start where you are and change the end.

—Often attributed to C.S. Lewis

Investment portfolios benefit from active management. This is true not only in public equity and hedge fund asset classes, but is equally important in private asset classes. This is not to contradict the point that consistency in commitments and relationships is very much at the core of manager selection. However, investment firms are living organisms that change over time and over the course of a 10- to 20-year relationship. Some firms have greater success building out their firms and instilling great confidence in the repeatability of their investment strategy, while others fall short. It is difficult to predict how firms will evolve, and mistakes in manager selection are inevitable.

Tool in Active Portfolio Management

Aside from the continual reassessment of the GP's capabilities, there are occasions that prompt institutional investors to redesign an asset class strategy and consider the role of each GP in the asset class portfolio. The most notable reasons are: (1) change in risk or liquidity tolerance of the

Table 10.1

Considerations for Secondary Sale
• Selection of a secondary agent
• Constructing the portfolio of funds for sale
• Pricing dynamics and transaction costs
• Risk management benefits against the cost

Source: The William and Flora Hewlett Foundation.

organization, (2) change of CIO, or (3) change in the director of the asset class. Typically, a fresh review of the program prompted by change in objective or staff will prompt a re-underwriting of every manager in the asset class portfolio. This usually results in a list of GP relationships that are determined to have an appropriate role in the portfolio, but perhaps need to be resized. It also results in a list of relationships that, for one reason or another, will no longer be continued. The CIO and asset class director are then faced with the decision of whether to hold the discontinued investment fund or sell the fund in a secondary sale transaction.

Typically, sales of private fund interests in the secondary market take place at a discount to the carrying value of the fund. The negative impact on one-year portfolio return resulting from a secondary sale must be weighed against potential underperformance of the asset class going forward. In many instances, the incentive compensation plan of the investment team will be impacted by the secondary sale and requires a thoughtful conversation regarding the expected benefits and cost. In short, a secondary sale is not a decision to be made lightly.

The primary areas to consider before engaging in a secondary transaction are listed on Table 10.1.

Broad adoption of private asset classes by pension plans, sovereign wealth funds, and family office portfolios over the past decade has enlarged the universe of potential sellers and buyers of private fund interests. This evolution has resulted in improved liquidity in secondary transactions allowing CIOs to actively manage private exposures across institutional portfolios in a more cost-efficient manner.

As the secondary market professionalized, the buyer universe grew from 20 to 80–90 buyers. Buyers of LP fund interests in secondary transactions are typically secondary funds raised for the sole purpose of acquiring a diversified pool of secondary LP interests on behalf of their clients. Secondary fund managers have both the staff resources and depth of experience to efficiently price and bid on portfolios of all sizes. More recently, large multi-product firms, sovereign wealth funds, and family offices have engaged as buyers of secondary transactions as a way to build a private investment portfolio with vintage-year diversification and to gain access to sought-after GPs.

To provide a sense of how the marketplace has expanded, in 2009 annual transactions in the secondary market across venture, buyout, real estate, and energy aggregated to $10 billion. A decade later, over $90 billion of secondary transactions closed. The sweet spot for deal size has also increased over the past decade from $150–$200 million, to $300–$500 million, in line with the increased size and pace of fund raising of secondary funds.

Fortunately, the broadening of the secondary market has made it somewhat less challenging to obtain the necessary approval to transfer LP interests to another investor. The level of activity has forced GPs to have a more efficient approval process that is handled by the operations teams at their firms. This is quite different from the ad hoc approval process prevalent a decade ago where the approval was handled by the managing partner. While the obstacle to receiving approval has diminished, GPs have also streamlined their side and perhaps provide approvals only once per quarter, instead of the flexibility provided in the past. Notwithstanding greater familiarity with secondaries, communicating intent to include their firm's fund in a secondary requires a great deal of relationship management.

Selection of a Secondary Agent

Boutique firms specializing in secondaries have built up staff in order to facilitate transactions and alleviate pressure on internal investment staff. Despite billions of dollars of secondary transactions over the past dozen years, there is no document standardization, making the process somewhat burdensome.

There are several things to consider when selecting a secondary agent; however, the first step is understanding if the secondary transaction firm only represents sellers, or whether they represent both buyers and sellers. A firm that only represents sellers is highly incentivized to maximize sale price for every transaction. Secondary agents that represent both buyers and sellers have the advantage of being able to serve as the single trusted partner for an investment program looking to transact on either the sale or purchase of secondary interests.

Selection of the secondary agent is typically handled by the private investment team in conjunction with the CIO and is best done using a framework that clearly states the objectives of the CIO in engaging the

Table 10.2

Secondary Firm Selection Criteria
• Capacity of the secondary firm to take on additional transactions
• Strength of the firm's relationships with GPs and secondary buyers
• Capacity of the firm's closing team
• A commitment to prioritize the engagement
• Speed at which the transaction can close
• Fees charged by the secondary agent

Source: The William and Flora Hewlett Foundation.

process. Simplifying the selection criteria on priorities for the organization is useful in assessing which firm can best complement the resources of the investment team in ensuring that the sales price is maximized and the organization is able to provide the necessary resources. The six typical areas to consider in selecting a secondary agent are listed on Table 10.2.

How an investment team weighs each of the six areas can vary, based on the capacity of the investment team and ability of the operations team to provide the not insignificant amount of documentation to the secondary firm's team.

Constructing a Portfolio for Sale

Whether a secondary sale is prompted by a change in strategy, change in asset class director or CIO, or disappointment with the GP's ability to execute strategy, thought needs to be given to the construction of the portfolio of funds to be offered up for sale.

There is no checklist an investor uses in constructing a secondary sales pool. For some investors, it is a risk-reduction exercise, for others the objective is time management of the staff, while for others it is to provide headroom for the new asset class director to shape the asset class portfolio toward the new strategy. The most challenging part of designing the portfolio for sale is the work required by the investment team to underwrite the expected go-forward return of each fund being considered for sale in order to arrive at the minimum reserve price. The team needs to consider whether the underlying assets have the potential to compound go-forward return at a rate that matches or exceeds the rate of return available from other opportunities competing for capital in the portfolio. The team must evaluate the underlying companies and assets, as well as consider the timing of distributions in making the assessment of the present value of each fund.

There is also no rule of thumb for the type of transaction that maximizes price. Market conditions tend to determine whether a focused single manager/fund sale or a diversified fund portfolio sale is preferable. During times of market stress there tend to be a greater number of single-fund, concentrated transactions where buyers can get greater certainty in underwriting a single fund and the underlying portfolio of assets. Conditions of uncertainty tend to result in demand for "mosaic" portfolios consisting of a handful of well-known managers/fund interests where buyers are typically adding to existing exposures in their fund portfolios.

During normal times, transactions consisting of pools of diversified funds are more common because buyers want the diversification benefit provided by a broad manager roster, and the diversification of vintage-year risk inherent in buying multiple funds of the same GP. In a portfolio sale, there is less granularity in underwriting of the intrinsic value of the individual portfolio holdings, and the dynamic can often reflect supply/demand of the asset class exposure. For this reason, the greater the number of funds and the higher quality of managers that can be included in a portfolio for sale, the greater the probability of multiple bidders and the greater the ability to meet the underwriting hurdle of the buyer.

Notably, secondary buyers prefer name-brand fund interests that are easier to underwrite and can prove helpful in attracting investors into their secondary funds. Buyers that can quickly perform due diligence on funds through an extensive database are best positioned to provide fair pricing to the seller and have greater certainty of closing the transactions. Eclectic or less-well-known manager interests take greater effort to underwrite, have greater uncertainty in underwriting, and therefore command heavier discounts to the last carrying value.

Pricing Dynamics

Pricing of secondary interests is largely determined by supply and demand. Typically, transaction volume is highest when there is a small spread between the price sellers are willing to accept, and the bid buyers are ready to make. The broadening of the buyer universe to secondary funds with fixed investment periods should underpin demand and allow equilibrium in bid-ask spreads to normalize over time.

Typically, it makes most sense to sell fund interests in the secondary market during the first quarter of a calendar year since budgets at funds that are purchasing secondary interests are at their highest early in the year. Demand is also highest following several years of strong asset class performance as institutions look to increase exposure to the asset class and secondary funds are eager to put money to work on behalf of their LPs. Conversely, it is difficult to maximize sales price during periods when there are many sellers in the market. Buyers often are willing to increase the stated sales price in exchange for delayed payment structures in which the seller provides financing for one or two years.

Buyer's bids reflect both the existing NAV of the fund plus the unfunded commitment remaining outstanding. Buyer's bids usually reflect the cash price at a discount (or premium) to the carrying value at a predetermined cut-off date, typically one or two quarters beforehand, plus or minus cash flows in the interim period. By the time a secondary transaction closes, the stated bid price may have a different discount from what was once calculated when the bid was received. Below is an example:

> In January 2022, a secondary pool receives a bid of 90% of the NAV at 9/30/21. The bid is accepted in February 2022 and the transaction is set to close May 2022. Between February and May of 2022, two quarterly valuation statements (12/31/21 and 3/31/22) are received and recorded by the operations team and are reflected in the updated NAV. If the quarterly valuations increased in value subsequent to 9/30/21, then the discount at which the secondary sale is occurring has widened. Of course, it is also possible the subsequent valuation statements reflect a decrease in value, in which case the discount narrows. In addition, there should be consideration of the opportunity cost of waiting for the sale to close.

Risk Management Benefits versus Cost

Advantages of using secondary sales to transition portfolios and manage endowment risk must be considered in light of the drawbacks to the long-term return of the endowment. The cost in terms of time, money, and relationships is a significant transaction cost in actively managing private investment portfolios. For this reason, successful institutions with stability in the CIO and investment team engage in secondary transactions perhaps only once or twice a decade.

Benefits

Risk reduction: Pruning is especially helpful in managing portfolio risk. The reality is that a successful venture and buyout program will out-earn every other asset class in the endowment. Over time, venture and buyout could consume much of the capital and risk budget of the portfolio. A well-timed and executed secondary sale allows the CIO to actively manage equity beta risk and illiquidity risk, and ensure the institution will not face funding risk.

Long-term outperformance of asset class: Investors need to consider whether the assets held in the underlying funds being considered for sale have the potential to outperform the asset class benchmark. Presumably, the funds included in the secondary sale have already been determined to have a low probability of beating the benchmark on a go-forward basis. By pruning low-performing funds the asset class portfolio has a higher probability of achieving superior returns over the long term.

Time management: Selling non-core interests relieves the private investment team from having to allocate time to the monitoring of funds. The challenge of monitoring funds with GPs that no longer consider the institution a "partner" can be difficult and is often left to the newer members of the private team. Instead, a well-designed sale allows the CIO and private team to develop and mentor younger team members while underwriting new funds and re-underwriting existing manager relationships.

Drawbacks

Immediate hit to return and reinvestment risk: If the secondary sale occurred at a discount to the NAV carrying value, the return of the portfolio will be impacted in the short term. Redeployment risk and the time expected to earn back the amount of the discount at sale need to be considered. Without a doubt, after a secondary sale is completed, the organization will have fewer assets invested in private assets with the potential of earning premium returns from illiquidity relative to public market alternatives.

Impact on incentive compensation: The team must consider and agree on the potential reduction in endowment alpha resulting from the secondary sale at a discount to the carrying value, and the consequences of it on the calculation of incentive bonus paid across the investment team.

Reputational risk: In a world with plenty of capital looking for investment in private asset classes, the competition for access to managers intensifies. Competitive peers could use knowledge of a secondary sale event against an institution in order to improve their allocations. It is critical that the market not know that the institution is selling.

11

Benchmarks

*You measure the size of your accomplishment by the obstacles you had
to overcome to reach your goals.*

—Booker T. Washington

Portfolio benchmarks are a critical component of dynamic investment management. The ability to measure the return of the investment portfolio against a pre-determined and agreed-upon set of benchmarks is key to understanding the sources of return and the skill of the investment team in delivering returns over the long term. Ideally, benchmarks should only change when there is a structural change in asset allocation or there is a specific concern about the reliability of an existing benchmark being used. For this reason, the review of portfolio benchmarks typically coincides with strategic asset allocation work.

The reason benchmark design occurs alongside asset allocation is that there is clarity at that moment in time about the policy portfolio objectives and the policy portfolio allocation to private assets. Therefore, having private asset allocation is not a risk solely borne by the CIO; it is instead shared by the CIO and the IC.

Traditionally, investment organizations sought to follow the basic principles of benchmarks set forth over 30 years ago by the CFA Institute. Table 11.1 lists the core principles to consider in selecting benchmarks.

Table 11.1

Principles of Benchmarks
• Be measured over time
• Measure the intended investment strategy
• Be investable
• Have the components known to the manager ahead of time

Source: The William and Flora Hewlett Foundation and CFA Institute.

Such criteria are inherently logical, and one can see how these criteria can be readily applied to investments that are highly liquid. However, it is equally clear that some of the ideal characteristics are unattainable when designing a benchmark for illiquid private fund investments. For example, private fund returns are reported quarterly with a meaningful lag, the component funds are not known in advance, and reflect a pooled stream of cash flows that an investor simply could not access in the aggregate. Accordingly, recognizing the limitations inherent in designing private asset benchmarks, this chapter presents additional details around design and testing of the appropriate benchmarks.

Benchmark Design Options

Benchmark design should at the highest level be focused on what the institution is trying to measure. Determining the purpose of the benchmark helps to guide the decision. In practice, the IC usually has two goals in mind: (1) to measure whether the annual return is adequate to sustain the real value of the endowment over the long term, and (2) to assess the value added by the investment team in selecting managers to execute our asset allocation strategy against the composite portfolio benchmark.

There are two methods of calculating composite portfolio benchmarks, each of which allows the IC to measure slightly different things:

1. Benchmark returns using *policy portfolio weights* for each of the underlying asset classes
2. Benchmark returns using *actual net asset value (NAV) weights* for each of the underlying asset classes

By using policy portfolio weighted benchmarks, the IC can measure the investment team's tactical asset allocation decisions, as well as manager selection. However, once the endowment has a significant deployment to illiquid assets, the investment team is limited by liquidity constraints in the ability to make tactical asset allocation decisions.

Benchmarks using actual net asset value weights for each asset class are typically used when the IC wants to isolate and measure the investment team's skill in manager selection and the implementation of strategies within each asset class.

There is no right answer for designing the appropriate benchmark for an endowment. Instead, every institution needs to take into account the responsibilities delegated to the investment team and to what extent there is joint ownership (between the investment committee and the CIO) of asset allocation.

The Delegation of Authority by the Hewlett IC to the CIO clearly communicates the joint ownership of the policy portfolio asset allocation. What is essential in maintaining trust between the CIO and the IC is the shared philosophy and framework around asset allocation and benchmarks and the commitment by the CIO that benchmarks are appropriate and will not be modified unless there is a structural shift in the portfolio.

There are several philosophies of benchmark design across the investment management industry. At the highest level, the framework can be considered along the lines of what is easily investable, and the opportunity set offered within a particular asset class. The variation in design is largely in the benchmarking of private investments. Table 11.2 summarizes the four benchmark methodologies currently employed by most large endowments and foundations.

The primary goal of Hewlett's benchmark design is to isolate skill in manager selection and execution of asset class strategy. At the beginning of the investment program, Hewlett's IC adopted the first methodology shown in Table 11.2, combining passive indices for public assets

Table 11.2

Benchmark Methodologies
1. A combination of passive indices for public assets and pooled-mean manager benchmarks for private assets
2. A simple passive public market, risk-based proxy, such as 70% MSCI World Equity Index and 30% Bloomberg US Aggregate Bond Index
3. A combination of passive indices for public assets and public market equivalent indices (PME) for private assets
4. A combination of passive indices for public assets and risk-premium-based calculations for private assets (e.g., MSCI World Equity Index + 400 basis points)

Source: The William and Flora Hewlett Foundation.

with pooled-manager benchmarks for private assets. We believe pooled-manager benchmarks most appropriately reflect the opportunity set and fundraising success of each private investment strategy across the globe. By using pooled-manager benchmarks, the IC is able to isolate the value added by the investment team in manager selection and strategy implementation. The benchmark is calculated using *actual net asset value (NAV) weights* for each of the underlying asset classes.

There are advantages and disadvantages to each of the methodologies. The simple passive 70/30 composite benchmark represents a low-cost way of earning market returns in the absence of an investment team. However, a portfolio invested across public and private asset classes would have periods of significant over/under performance simply due to timing of private marks. The PME-based calculations aim to address the timing difference inherent in private investing by adjusting contributions and distributions of capital. The PME methodology suffers from two drawbacks: a potential for significant mismatch in the underlying beta of the public and private cash flows and the fact that asset class PMEs are not provided by an independent third party. The fourth methodology mentioned measures whether the institution was paid for taking illiquidity risk. Over a decade or more, this methodology may prove useful; however, in shorter time periods the episodic return profile of private investments may result in significant over/under performance.

There are some institutions of higher learning that incorporate peer benchmarks as part of the review of the skill added by the investment team. There are two key drawbacks to using peer comparison of investment returns: (1) the conversation about return does not include conversation about the risk (volatility, illiquidity, leverage, etc.) an institution took to achieve the reported investment return, and (2) the performance competition hurts collaboration among endowments and foundations that should be helping each other achieve superior returns.

Further complicating the design of reported benchmarks and comparison of returns among peers is the lag in reporting by private funds. Typically, private funds report returns between 60 and 90 days after the end of each quarter. This compares to monthly returns calculated by public asset managers. Some institutions calculate and report the return of the endowment with a one-quarter lag, while others delay reporting return until all private fund reports have been received. While reporting should be footnoted, it seldom is included in press reports or reports generated by data providers.

Benchmark Selection

The objective of selecting appropriate asset class benchmarks is to allow the measurement of the investment team's ability to select managers and implement strategies within each asset class. They reflect the strategy and risk of each asset class in the portfolio. In addition, appropriate benchmarks allow the investment team to measure the realized active risk resulting from a series of individual fundamentally driven decisions made on a bottom-up basis.

The CIO needs to consider how the asset class benchmark is designed, how the data is collected and return calculated, and the coverage of the universe. For example, MSCI World Index covers around 85% of the free-float adjusted market capitalization in each of the 23 countries included. The index measures price performance and income from dividend payments. The Burgiss Buyout Index calculates returns from data compiled from over 3,700 funds raised over 40 years.

The best approach for measuring the investment team's skill in alternative asset classes is the use of a manager-pooled mean benchmark, under the theoretical assumption the organization could earn this return by investing passively in every manager in the asset class. The pooled mean calculation aggregates the cash flows and ending market values from all funds represented in an index, and then calculates the IRR of the entire stream. One can conceptualize this effort as the "total market return" of an asset class, which can serve as the best representation of the beta. The use of manager population benchmarks allows the team to evaluate the returns of similarly structured funds dedicated to a similar investment opportunity.

Testing the Benchmarks

On a practical level, the CIO must be able to defend the accuracy of the data underlying the benchmarks since they are used not only for reporting to stakeholders, but also in the calculation of incentive pay for the investment team. For this reason, selecting a private asset benchmark provider requires the investment team to test the consistency of the data, as well as the impact of reporting and survivorship bias in the return series generated by the provider.

There are several providers of private fund benchmarks. Some use return data provided by the investment funds, while others use the data provided by the client's capital account statements. It is challenging to test benchmark data when managers choose whether to report returns. The magnitude of the bias differs depending on the breadth of the manager universe, the consistency of the benchmark provider's client base (since they populate the database), treatment of cash flows and currency variation, and the methodology by which each provider handles fund inclusion and departures.

The appropriateness of a given benchmark for the investment program can be tested by observing the correlation of the portfolio's *realized* returns by asset class to the asset class benchmarks over a 10-year period. Ideally, the realized return of the public asset portfolio has a correlation of 0.9–1.0 to their respective benchmarks. Realized returns in private asset classes typically have correlations of 0.8–0.9 to their respective benchmarks.

Making Changes to Benchmarks

Benchmark changes should only be proposed when there is data that shows the current benchmark is no longer "appropriate," or there is a more accurate benchmark service provider available, or there is a change in asset class designations. For full transparency, the investment team should present the impact of the change in benchmark as if it had been done retroactively and be able to provide the IC with information about the extent to which the change in benchmarks could be material in calculation of the excess return of the portfolio.

The risk in making changes to the benchmark is that the IC and board have the opportunity to question whether the change proposed will favor the investment team compensation program. Investors should balance the materiality of a change in benchmark against the potential skepticism of the compensation committee and the IC. If the impact of the proposed change is not material or warranted by an event (change in benchmark provider or asset class designation), it is preferable to just leave benchmarks unchanged.

From Second Camp to Third Camp

The trajectory between second camp and third camp requires a different set of skills from what was required to arrive at second camp. Unlike the ascent to second camp, which required significant technical skills, the climb to third camp requires much softer skills. Similar to the challenge of ascending the large, exposed sections of the mountain typical of the climb between second camp and third camp, the expedition team is faced with the challenge of making decisions on the investment managers and funds that will significantly impact the course of the portfolio.

Manager selection is a difficult and challenging activity that at times feels like crossing a narrow and steep ridge with steep drops on either side. Moving forward at this altitude requires the success of the managers and partners selected for the climb. Conducting due diligence and learning how to monitor the portfolio are the key areas for successfully arriving at third camp. The investment team must be keenly aware of the values and culture they have created in order to be able to draw upon those factors as they push further up the mountain.

It is through first-hand experience of knowing what it takes to make a successful investor and investment team that the team is then able to judge and select the investment partners for the climb to third camp. An investment team that is able to adapt the lessons learned along the ascent, from base camp through second camp, to identify the skills and shortcomings of other investors, should have greater success in aggregating a group of truly superior managers. Innately, the investment team should know which partners to trust and which partners are not aligned in their objective. As the altitude weighs the body and muscles down, the allocator expedition team and the GP expedition team are able to help each other to achieve the same goal.

As the team ascends to third camp it may want to move more aggressively to the summit. While the weather and terrain are unpredictable, there is a sense that perhaps too much time was spent preventing bad things from happening and the team could have made more progress. Of course, the oxygen in the air is also thinning at this higher altitude, so perhaps part of the relief is simply that the portfolio successfully withstood several challenges. Navigating through difficult periods and pushing forward during periods of clear skies has undoubtedly taught every member of the team new skills.

Upon arriving at a rocky outcrop to rest, it becomes obvious to the team that there really are only two types of investors/climbers – those who accept that losses are part of the game and those that refuse to accept they make mistakes. The successful expedition team learns there is no way to prevent bad events and instead dedicates precious energy to improving resilience and limiting damage.

12

Manager Selection

When it came time for each of us to assess our own abilities and weigh them against the formidable challenge of the world's highest mountain, it sometimes seemed as though half the population at Base Camp was clinically delusional. But perhaps this shouldn't have come as a surprise.
—John Krakauer, *Into Thin Air*[1]

While, on the surface, manager selection sounds fairly easy, it is not. Every investment manager believes they have the talent and skills to be a great investor and build a top-performing investment firm. As the quote above astutely notes, the investing world has its fair share of people who are eternal optimists, and perhaps, delusional. The job of the expedition team is to carefully select the partners for the ascent to the summit.

The ability to identify, gain access, and perform due diligence on outstanding GPs is typically the primary activity of an investment team. Through successful manager selection, the investment program is able to generate consistent alpha and deliver returns above the expected return of the policy portfolio. Managing internal portfolio risk begins with manager selection and is complemented by ongoing monitoring of every investment decision.

---

[1] Jon Krakauer, *Into Thin Air* (New York: Knopf Doubleday Publishing Group, 1998).

In many organizations, the identification of the strategic objective and opportunity set is guided by the CIO, while the selection of managers is the primary responsibility of the asset class specialists. Selecting a diverse group of managers within an asset class provides the portfolio with diversified sources of market beta and alpha. At the end of every manager selection process, both the CIO and the asset class director need to have a high degree of confidence in the investment.

The process of conducting diligence on a manager is how the asset class director comes to understand how the investment manager sources opportunities, underwrites investments, and sizes each investment within the fund portfolio. Through the process, the CIO and team should come to understand how the managing partners at the GP make decisions, admit mistakes, recruit and develop talent, and align incentives to promote a healthy culture.

Finally, manager selection needs to be approached as the core activity and an essential part of the culture of the investment team. A team culture that values intellectual curiosity and rigor in diligence is more likely to embrace a selection and monitoring process than not. When the process is embedded in culture, the investment team is able to identify blind spots and embedded biases, and importantly is able to pattern-match across multiple fund-raising cycles and managers. Successful investors know that it is by gathering insights across hundreds of diligence processes that they become better investors.

Evolution of Manager Selection

Manager selection has evolved as the proliferation of endowments, foundations, family offices, sovereign-wealth funds, and hospital systems, coupled with wide adoption of endowment-style investment programs, created the career of institutional allocators of capital. The CIOs of 20–30 years ago came from a diverse set of backgrounds, including banks, investment firms, and treasury departments. They learned first-hand what attributes made successful investors, portfolio managers, and investment firms. Since then, the majority of investment teams have been allocators of capital for their entire careers (post banking or business school). Most have not had direct investment experience or had to face first-hand the complexity that comes with implementing a portfolio and answering to clients. This evolution makes the due diligence process more important to generating superior returns over the long term.

For decades, many pools of capital managed by committees were guided by consultants using a "fill-in-the-box" approach to selecting investment managers. For example, they recommended hiring a value manager to counterbalance a growth manager or to balance the exposure of a large buyout manager with a small buyout manager. However, over the past two decades successful investment programs have evolved to be more strategic in assembling a collection of managers within an asset class.

Setting the Bar

A new investment program requires skills and enthusiasm for identifying managers, screening new firms, and underwriting every aspect of a new firm. This includes finding the resources to have operational and legal due diligence that can keep pace with the activity of the investment team. The CIO and investment team investing a new portfolio spend most of their time gaining access and getting to know managers. The bar or hurdle for a new manager in a new investment program is typically lower than the bar in a mature portfolio. In part, this is due to the fact that a new investment team is setting the hurdle as the team develops the strategy of the portfolio. A new portfolio may not have access to the caliber of managers included in the roster of mature investment programs. In effect, a new portfolio may invest in an A-rated team taking advantage of a B-rated opportunity set, or invest in a B-rated team in an A-rated opportunity set. This is part of the process of building a portfolio and over time gaining access to the type of managers the investment team believes will lead to superior investment returns.

In contrast, a mature portfolio has a very high bar for a new manager and adds a new manager only when they identify a new A-rated team with a strategy focused on an A-rated opportunity set. For this reason, most mature portfolios hire less than a handful of new managers each year across all asset classes, and the hurdle to be one of those few is very high. In mature portfolios, the investment team is principally re-underwriting every existing manager every couple of years to ensure that the firm remains healthy, and the opportunity set and strategy are aligned with the institution's objectives. The CIO and investment team investing a mature portfolio spend most of their time building and strengthening relationships with the GPs to ensure the health of the investment firm. These teams spend a great deal of time understanding the dynamics of the underlying portfolio companies to gain insights into quality of underwriting by the GPs. Monitoring the investment closely helps to surface issues that may warrant the end of the relationship with a GP.

Refining the Skills Needed on the Team

The skill sets needed to build a portfolio differ from those necessary to manage a mature portfolio. When a portfolio is in build mode, sourcing deals and being able to quickly underwrite are key skills to have on the team. In contrast, a mature portfolio needs skills in relationship management, portfolio management, and ability to understand the execution of strategy by analyzing the underlying assets of the fund. The primary activity of the team managing a mature portfolio is communicating with the manager in order to pick up on things happening either at the investment firm or at the portfolio companies. Sourcing new funds is a secondary activity.

It is important to take into consideration that there may be a point in the development of the investment program when some of the team who built the portfolio may no longer be the best skilled at managing a mature portfolio. An investor who finds joy in the discovery of a new idea or new manager is rarely the investor who finds joy in rolling up their sleeves in portfolio management and tracking the growth of cash flows at the portfolio asset level. Being able to recommend the termination of an investment manager is a skill necessary for a team managing a mature portfolio. On a practical level, an investor who enjoys sourcing new managers is likely to grow resentful in an organization with a mature portfolio since the frequency of being turned down on new manager suggestions would prove demoralizing.

Due Diligence Process Design

The objective of the due diligence process is to underwrite how an investment manager creates value over time and to assess the investment firm's philosophy and strategy. In addition, due diligence needs to culminate in an understanding of the investment firm's partners and the viability/ trajectory of the investment firm. Many investors approach this activity with a groan and use checklists that frequently miss larger issues. While checklists can be useful in ensuring all diligence items are covered, if an investor is focused on getting items checked off they may not be listening to the manager for clues that perhaps contradict key areas deemed important by the organization.

Diligence is not a process just for the sake of process. It anchors decisions and provides documentation of the rationale behind investment decisions that is useful for the organization. There is no single "right" way to design a due diligence and manager selection process; however, there are basic building blocks to consider in the design, as shown in Table 12.1.

Some organizations take comfort in creating 40-page memos because it forces the underwriting team to be thorough in diligence. Other investment offices just presume the thorough diligence is done and in the file for reference, and instead distill the memo to a handful of pages highlighting the strategy that is expected to create value and the competitive edge of the investment firm. Successful investment teams have designed due diligence processes that hold themselves to the same exacting standards they expect their managers to complete before they invest the organization's capital.

Manager Diligence and Selection Process

The manager selection process starts with due diligence of a new or existing manager. There are distinct stages to the process, starting with responsibility for triaging new investment opportunities. At this stage the asset class team determines if the manager has a clear competitive edge and identifies the market opportunity the manager hopes to capture. Assuming there is a valid competitive edge and the opportunity set is attractive, then the asset class team must determine how the manager being considered differs from existing managers in the portfolio and how the manager would fit into delivering the market beta and alpha expected from the asset class.

Table 12.1

Due Diligence Process Considerations
• Systematic process for triaging new investment funds/managers
• Due diligence process for new firms versus existing firm re-underwriting of new commitments
• Key areas to diligence and deliverables
• Degree of participation by CIO in due diligence
• Degree of team participation in diligence and manager selection

Source: The William and Flora Hewlett Foundation.

Once the asset class team and CIO have determined there is merit to pursuing the opportunity, then the team assembles a plan of action for comprehensive due diligence. Typically, this involves several on-site visits at the potential manager's office by the investment team to understand the manager's strategy, meet several levels of the GP team, and conduct operational due diligence.

Whether it is a new underwriting or the re-underwriting of a commitment to an existing manager, it is important that the questions shown in Table 12.2 be considered. Spending the time getting to know the motivation and passion of the GPs is essential in judging integrity and alignment. Understanding how the management fee, carry split, waterfall, key person, leverage, and portfolio construction make sense for the strategy and the firm are key considerations in selecting managers.

At Hewlett, we call this stage "The Four Ps." This refers to our work in assessing the firm's philosophy, process, people, and performance. Performance is intentionally the last element considered. We focus on the quality of the firm and the quality of the underlying assets and portfolio companies. Table 12.2 provides a starting list of questions to assess a GP's ability to generate consistent excess return.

When the diligence process is embedded in the culture of the investment team, the natural curiosity of the team will drive the conversation with the GP to the critical issues. The values of the investment team inevitably shape the view of the type of manager that would fit as a long-term partner of the organization. Not every firm culture will be a fit, and that is not a reflection of the manager quality or track record; it just doesn't fit the role or provide a degree of complementarity with the existing manager roster to warrant the addition to the portfolio.

Successful investors approach due diligence and manager selection with a ton of humility. It is impossible from the outside to know everything about an investment firm or predict how the partners will act when things go south (in markets there are always challenging periods). Regardless of how many decades of experience the investment team has, the investment team is usually surprised that they "miss" a key element. After decades of pattern matching, it is fair to say that allocators must understand that investment firms evolve, and sometimes the investment firm makes choices that serve them well but no longer make sense for the LPs. Mistakes in manager selection happen. What is important is to create an environment of trust within the investment team where every manager decision can be discussed and there is safety in pointing out issues of concern.

Table 12.2 The Four Ps of Diligence

Philosophy

- How do they create value?
- How do they source new investment ideas/deals?
- How do they construct the portfolio?
- How do they use leverage?
- Is the investment process consistently applied across all partners and products?
- Is there consistency in deals/positions?
- Has the firm strategy drifted over time?
- What is the risk of execution of the strategy?

Process

- How repeatable and disciplined is the investment process?
- What is the approach to drive change and capture return?
- Does the GP have sell discipline?
- Does the GP know when to walk away from an investment to avoid throwing good money after bad?
- Do they have differentiated viewpoints?
- What is the experience of the decision makers through market cycles?
- Is there clarity in decision making and sizing of investments?
- Do we like the assets they buy?
- How is the underwriting differentiated from other GPs in the asset class?
- Can the strategy generate consistent long-term returns?
- Can the process meet our strict diligence standards?
- Do they have deep domain expertise?
- Do they have solid relationships with banks and private credit lenders?
- Does the reputation of the firm help source investments or recruit talent?
- What is the risk management process?
- What are valuation procedures?

People

- What is the character of the GPs?
- Have they been thoughtful in building and developing their team?
- What is the strategy of ownership over time and sharing of carry?
- Does the GP do everything they can to recover value of investments that have not worked out?
- What is the vision for the firm?
- How do they define the culture of the firm?
- Are the values of the firm aligned with our values?
- Is the GP transparent in admitting mistakes?
- Alignment of incentives between GP and LPs?
- How transparently and frequently do they communicate with LPs?

(continued)

Table 12.2   (*Continued*)

- Is there clarity in decision making on firm issues?
- Can the firm scale? What are the plans for growing fund size?

Performance

- Is there consistency in generating superior returns (batting average, upside/downside capture)?
- What is the value bridge analysis to attribute steps in the value-creation tool kit?
- Have successful deals/positions been done by a couple of partners or by a broad set of partners?
- Is the historical track record generated by people still making investment decisions at the firm?

Source: The William and Flora Hewlett Foundation.

Being realistic helps. No matter how much effort is made by the investment team, more often than anyone would admit we get it wrong either in the assessment of the firm or the opportunity set. When the opportunity set turns out to be wrong, it is likely that there was a regulatory or geopolitical factor the team did not foresee. More frequently, the mistake is in underestimating the difficulty in executing the strategy set out by the GP. Other sources of error that are tough to identify, despite the hours of diligence and questions noted earlier in the chapter, are the manager's ability to continually recruit and retain top talent, the firm's ability to scale and execute the strategy as assets under management grow, and the founding partners' willingness to share ownership and carry as responsibilities in the firm broaden to other senior leaders.

From the outset, allocators accept that many decisions will be made with limited information. Throwing more data into a due diligence process doesn't always prove useful, and sometimes investors take comfort in having lots of data even when the data falls short of providing insight. Data rooms are only helpful in that they provide as much data as the GP wants LPs to have and is presented in a manner that typically favors the GP's results. Successful investors know the data is only the beginning of the process to understand how the returns were generated and to gain confidence in the probability the returns can be generated in the future.

Beyond the data, the decision to hire/commit to a manager, especially in private vehicles, comes down to trust. The CIO has to trust that the manager's value system is aligned with the organization's. The investment manager is trusted to build the culture of the firm in a way that retains talent and also maximizes the probability of success. LPs expect their roster of GPs to help portfolio companies grow and scale their businesses. It seems only appropriate that investment teams take into consideration how the GP has thought about building their own investment businesses in judging whether they are adding value on the portfolio company boards they serve.

Manager selection in private investment funds differs from selection in public investment classes such as hedge funds, public equities, and fixed income. The primary difference is that mistakes in the selection of managers can be fixed in liquid asset classes. A public manager can be resized (up or down) or terminated if they fail to deliver on expected return, or the long-term viability of the firm comes into question. The investments are relatively liquid and redeemable in three years or less, and the cost of discontinuing a public manager is low. This is in sharp contrast to private investment vehicles in venture, buyout, real estate, infrastructure, and energy. Mistakes in manager selection also occur in these asset classes, yet the cost of fixing mistakes is much greater (refer to Chapter 10 on secondaries). Since the cost of being wrong is higher, the hurdle for adding a new private manager and underwriting a follow-on commitment to an existing manager is higher in private assets than in public asset classes.

Despite the differences between selection of public and private selection of managers, there should be consistency in the investment team's due diligence underwriting across asset classes. Establishing clear and uniform standards for monitoring existing managers in the endowment should be ingrained into team culture. There should also be a repeatable process from the point at which the asset class considers a new opportunity to the CIO signing legal documents for new investments.

Finally, positioning the portfolio for the future requires the CIO to adapt to the manager selection process. Depending on the strategic direction of the portfolio, a CIO may encourage the team to search for niche strategies and specialist managers, while another CIO may focus efforts on creating a farm team manager roster. Adapting the manager selection process is a way to ensure the team is focusing on the areas that will allow the portfolio to outperform over the next decade.

Sizing the Investment

Once the assessment of the manager has concluded, then investors have to assess how the strategy and manager fit into the portfolio. The investment case includes a discussion of expected return and potential risks, including exogenous event risks that could impact the risk-reward framework. The CIO needs to be able to size the investment, taking into account the role the GP's strategy and opportunity play within the asset class and the aggregate endowment. Sizing of commitments is often based on the level of conviction, range of potential outcomes, and illiquidity profile. The CIO typically makes a judgment based on their confidence in the probability that the manager will execute the strategy and generate alpha.

Sizing also takes into consideration the pacing of subsequent fund raises by the manager. The team typically models out the future exposure to a single GP across various funds, taking into account distributions and outperformance of the GP relative to the overall portfolio. Managing the level of unfunded commitments relative to the NAV is a challenge faced by every investment team. There are "rules of thumb" developed over the years that serve as a guide for sizing commitments (refer to Chapter 9).

Lastly, an element of sizing is sometimes beyond the control of the institution and based on the attractiveness of the LP as a client of the GP. This may sound odd, but the most sought-after managers, in both private and public asset classes, have limited capacity. In effect, this means LPs are competing for allocations to funds, and sizing is the result of a decision made by the GP of the amount the LP is "asked" to commit.

Monitoring the Portfolio

Ongoing monitoring through frequent communication with investment partners is necessary to evaluate whether each manager is executing the strategy as underwritten and whether the strategy is efficiently delivering returns. Investors must pay particular attention to the development of a firm's investment team, the appropriateness of asset size and growth, and the characteristics of the underlying portfolio in evaluating the conviction level and appropriate sizing of the investment.

Developing a process for monitoring the existing portfolio provides clarity and direction for the investment team. Typically, the responsibilities for monitoring include the review of the quarterly letters; GP communication through letters, blogs, and quarterly/semi-annual calls; and attending the annual meeting.

Monitoring the portfolio goes deeper than reading or listening to the official messages from GPs. Having 36 years of experience as a GP and an LP has helped me build trusting relationships with many of the managers in the Hewlett portfolio. Many of our managers are comfortable calling for advice in difficult times, and we can provide support and encouragement when their strategy is not working (nearly all strategies face moments when they hit a wall).

At Hewlett, the asset class team spends several months each year thinking strategically about the asset class they oversee. The discipline of deep dives into each asset class provides the team with a valuable opportunity to evaluate the strategy, portfolio construction, and contribution of the asset class to the overall portfolio. In public asset classes, the team re-underwrites each of the managers every couple of years to assess whether the original premise of the investment remains valid and whether the execution of the strategy has gone according to plan. In private asset classes, the cadence of fund raising by the GPs essentially forces a new re-underwriting of every manager every few years.

The objective of ongoing assessments of existing GPs in a mature portfolio is to identify factors that either increase or decrease the conviction level in the GP's ability to generate excess return. Similarly, when a new CIO and investment team inherit a mature portfolio, every single manager must be underwritten to make a fresh assessment of the role they could play in the organization's investment portfolio.

The expectation of higher returns in illiquid structures should be balanced against the risk of errors in manager selection or the manager's failure to execute a strategy, especially since we invest in funds that last 10–12 years. Absolute confidence in manager selection is difficult since, despite the best efforts of the team, sometimes the analysis turns out to be wrong, or the manager decision was sound, but the market environment did not allow the manager to meet return expectations. The cost to the portfolio of an underperforming manager/strategy is higher in private assets since the capital is "locked up" for the remaining life of the fund (plus extensions). While secondary sales are tools to manage the portfolio, transactions typically involve a discount to carrying value and should be minimized where possible.

Identifying Biases in Mature Portfolios

A necessary part of portfolio management is patience and the curiosity to dig and understand why a manager may be underperforming or why a particular strategy failed to achieve the expected results. In public asset classes, managers typically blame underperformance on "the market" or on "style rotation" when more often than not, the root cause is poor bond or stock selection. In private asset classes. GPs typically blame the management team at the underlying portfolio company or the economic cycle, instead of their own errors in underwriting or failure to help the company or asset achieve the underwriting plan.

Many investors attribute their success to discipline. In the investment world, discipline is very important in acknowledging bias and incorporating behavioral traits into decisions. While books have been written about the various biases that exist in the investing world, the following are the six most common biases to guard against in evaluating a mature portfolio.

Survivorship bias: Overestimating the chances of success because the portfolio has generated good returns and there are more stories of successful allocators than failed ones.

Sunk-cost fallacy: Unwillingness to quit a manager or strategy because the team has spent a great deal of time and effort in the attempt to improve return outlook. The time and capital spent in a decision that for a number of reasons has ended poorly should play no role in the decision to sell. Only the future return of the asset or fund, and the future performance relative to other assets, should be considered.

Story bias: It is natural to want to believe the stories of success provided by our managers. However, narratives give us a false sense that we understand an investment and inevitably lead us to take greater risks, especially when data and evidence are thin. After all, depending on how something is framed, and by whom, we are pre-conditioned to believe it.

Circle of knowledge: This is sometimes most difficult for investors to avoid because it demands that we at times accept what we do not know. Being self-aware to know where your knowledge ends is key, and requires humility.

Outcome bias: This is a very difficult bias to overcome because investors are laser-focused on generating returns. However, assessing the result or the return based on the outcome, instead of the process used to obtain the result, misses a great deal of potential learning. Consistently superior returns require a repeatable process.

To be sure, every investor has biases. They are neither good or bad. As a team, it is important to be aware of these biases and assess whether they have in fact resulted in superior decision making and returns. It also makes sense to examine the manager roster and assess whether there is a bias that runs across the portfolio, and then figure out if it is material and should be corrected.

At Hewlett, several years ago we engaged in the exercise of examining whether there was a bias running across the entire portfolio. What we realized was that the main GP/portfolio manager in nearly every invest-ment we had made was between 40 and 50 years of age. To the point that a bias doesn't always need to be corrected, we did not intentionally go out and search for a new roster of GPs that were outside that age range. Instead, we elevated understanding strategic evolution of a firm's owner-ship and decision-making process as a higher priority during diligence and monitoring.

Knowing When to Quit

Despite best efforts at controlling the outcome, not every decision turns out to be right either because the opportunity set changed, the manager focus shifted, or the manager was unable to execute the strategy as it was originally underwritten. There is rarely an "aha" moment when the CIO or the investment team knows it is time to walk away from an existing manager. It is a process of discovery and a process that is best done work-ing together as a team to protect the portfolio from unintended bias.

The following are three examples of how the evolution of the firm or opportunity set may be reason enough to walk away.

In the first example, we compare two firms and judge them on the approach each took to building the investment firm. Firm A intention-ally mentors and identifies high-potential associates early in their careers. They recruit and retain a deep bench of principals and VPs that have been promoted to MDs. The path to promotion is clear. In contrast, firm B spun out of a traditional buyout shop. Over time it became clear the three founding partners believed they did not need to hire the quality of peo-ple necessary to build the next generation of investors at the firm. There was an unclear path to promotion, and the partners were not generous in sharing carry (let alone ownership in the firm). Their greed extended to aspirations of ever-larger fund size and assets under management. We do not worry about the long-term viability of Firm A. A lack of conviction on the long-term viability of Firm B caused us to step away.

In the second example, we compare two firms on their ability to foresee and adapt to significant changes in the sectors of focus for their strategy. Firm X raised multiple funds based on a successful strategy of acquiring older businesses where the market mispriced the asset value because they "misjudged" the pace of decline of the revenue stream. In the analysis of the most recent fund, it became evident that they fell short of anticipating the speed of disruption to the revenue stream at nearly all of the portfolio companies in the fund. Being wrong happens, and if it happens in one or maybe two portfolio companies in a fund, the errors can be overcome. When it happens at the core of the underwriting model across nearly every investment in a single fund, the fund return will be severely impacted. Failure to accept changes in the underwriting model became the core area of concern. In contrast, Firm Y built a narrow-sector firm and over the course of multiple funds realized that they needed to adapt their strategy based on the economic cycle. This firm was transparent with LPs and successfully argued that flexibility in capital allocation among subsectors would be required to achieve the expected return objective. The GP invested in hiring highly talented investors in each of the subsectors, while ensuring all of the specialists were compensated on the carry of the entire fund. In this case, the GP placed the interests of the LPs ahead of the cost to the firm of adapting the strategy.

The third example of a manager mistake is less frequent since it involves unforeseen regulatory changes. In this case, the GP raised a fund to invest in a new business model resulting from disruption. Unfortunately, two years into the investment period there was a landmark legal decision invalidating the business model. When a regulatory event occurs that makes the continuation of a firm's strategy impossible, the GP faces choices. The GP can pivot and invest capital in something that resembles the original strategy while attempting to salvage value in the investments already made, or the GP can stop the investment period. Unfortunately, the firm did not cease the investment period and instead called the remaining committed capital in part to salvage value and in part to fund the existing operations of the firm. In this case, the GP chose to protect the viability of the firm instead of preserving the capital of its investors.

Consistently selecting managers who are able to consistently generate alpha for the endowment is very hard. Consistently picking excellent managers year after year is something every allocator aspires to. It is easy to do it once or twice and think that you know how to do it. Be humble because there is so much out of your control.

What makes it so hard? It is rarely obvious. The team and the asset class director have already invested so much time and energy into strengthening the relationship with the GP that the "easy" decision is to keep going. The decision with managers is eerily similar to the decision alpinists face on the mountain – press forward or turn back? Does the manager have enough fuel (risk) to make it? Will the weather (environment) hold? These are the moments when the experience and wisdom of the expedition veterans are critical in helping the asset class lead arrive at a decision.

There are two layers to evaluate; one is the investment firm, and the other is the investment strategy. An allocator of capital must have confidence in the behavior of the investment manager in good and bad times, and in the investment firm's ability to execute the strategy they think generates strong returns. Add behavioral psychology at each level (the management of the portfolio company, the investment firm team, and the different expectations of LPs) plus volatile financial markets and the degree of difficulty expands. Layer into the mix the role the GP has in the portfolio and the impact of changes in the needs of the organization, cash flows, and risk contribution from other asset classes. Knowing when to quit is hard. Know that allocators are rarely right every time they hire or end a relationship with a manager.

You don't have to be right all the time. I have made plenty of mistakes picking managers. Sometimes it is the manager, sometimes it is the environment, and sometimes the needs of the portfolio changed. The process should be consistent because the outcome rarely is. The process by which you make the decision to quit should also be considered, because it will take much of the drama out of the decision. In the end, it is important to remember that challenging experiences are important lessons and the experiences shared ultimately strengthen the team.

Part III

THE SUMMIT IN VIEW

Reaching for the Summit

For the first time on the expedition, the vista was primarily sky rather than earth.

—John Krakauer, *Into Thin Air*[1]

In the ascent from third camp to the summit, the strength of relationships – between the IC and board, the expedition team, and the managers/GPs – provides the sustenance for the last push against the elements. Investing time in strengthening communication and relationship with the IC and board becomes crucial when the expedition faces challenges and "radios" down for help. Likewise, the strength of the bond among the team, and the respect and trust in the leader's courage to make difficult decisions, helps to ensure success. Finally, prioritizing relationships with other climbers (managers and peers) means learning from them best practices and cultural values that can strengthen the team.

The path from third and final camp to the summit is referred to as "the death zone" because it is the easiest place to lose focus. The thin air creates hallucinations and euphoria. There is a spot along the way where alpinists reach the "south summit" and can almost taste victory. This joy is quickly dampened when approaching an unexpected gap in the relationship with a board, team member, or manager that causes dread and despair. No matter how close an expedition or an investment team gets to the summit, conditions can change, and new obstacles appear. An expedition team with strong discipline, driven by passion and vision, can overcome the perils at this extreme altitude.

Keeping the team focused and disciplined at all times is the only way to reach the summit. The expedition team respects and trusts that the leader will know when to turn back. Knowing when to quit is important when conditions change or members of the team exhibit signs of distress and the team must find a different way forward. Difficult decisions require great courage and forgoing the promise of the summit is disappointing. However, a strong leader is able to encourage the team to try making the ascent to the summit at a later time when the probability of success has improved.

In this final push to the summit, many investors fall short and lose their balance and perspective. It is the combination of thin air and severe weather that causes alpinists to lose their sense of direction. The best way to

---

[1] Jon Krakauer, *Into Thin Air* (New York: Knopf Doubleday Publishing Group, 1998).

combat succumbing to disorientation near the summit is to have a trusted group of climbers alongside you on the ascent, keeping your feet firmly on the ground. The interdependence among the team and the reliance upon the IC and the investment managers for safety and success unify and protect everyone's safety and the success of the investment program. It also helps greatly if there is a deep commitment to a mission and serving others.

The discipline required to become an excellent investor and reach the summit consumes your life. You have to have a passion for investing to be great at this job. The more time you invest in your career, the higher you can climb. It is a choice how high up the mountain you want to climb, and the trade-offs required to achieve the goal are consequences of choices made. I am fortunate to have a family that is supportive of my career and the 24/7 demands of the job. My husband and kids understand that as important as they are in my life, my commitment to work is equally important. Reaching the summit has meant I missed birthdays, anniversaries, and recitals because work-related trips took precedence. I made sure that the moments I did spend with my family, I was present for them. My husband was amazing at shielding me from the guilt because he had every situation with the kids handled. As adults, my three kids appreciate having a parent with dedication to the craft of investing because they have a model of how they hope to shape their professional careers.

Perhaps it is the thin air or the bitter cold wind at the summit that fills the expedition team with an immense amount of gratitude – for the organization, for their fellow climbers, and for the managers. As the team prepares for the descent, it is important to acknowledge the board and IC for the encouragement, support, and financing of the expedition team from base camp all the way to the summit. Appreciation for the faith they maintained in the expedition team when at times it must have felt nerve-wracking as storm clouds gathered on the mountain and the summit itself became impossible to see.

As every experienced climber realizes all too soon after reaching the summit, the descent is equally treacherous. Not only are the weather conditions and technical challenges still there on the way down the mountain, but the team is exhausted, and food and fuel start to run out. Lethargy begins to set in. Most dangerous during the descent from the summit is that a single careless step can endanger the team. The team's skills are put to the test during the descent from the summit in ways they hadn't experienced during the ascent. The two factors that many climbers attribute to having survived the descent from the summit are their internal drive to survive and the bond with their fellow climbers.

These final four chapters focus on the importance of relationships, and the role of courage and trust. Without these, the ascent to the summit would feel hollow. Reaching the summit is rarely done alone. It takes intentionality to design and manage an excellent, high-performing investment team that trusts each other and enjoys spending time together. Finally, the ascent to the summit reaffirms purpose. That may sound odd since ascending to the summit was the entire purpose of the expedition. Yet, once an investor is at the summit, there is truly no alternative but climbing the next mountain. Fortunately, capital markets change frequently enough during an investor's career that finding a new challenging mountain to climb and summit is the natural next step.

13

Managing the Team

Climb the mountain not to plant your flag, but to embrace the challenge, enjoy the air and behold the view. Climb it so you can see the world, not so the world can see you.

—David McCullough Jr.[1]

The CIO as expedition leader is delegated a significant amount of responsibility to ensure the institution can meet its goal of reaching the summit. Key to delivering on this objective is the effective management of the team and a proper incentive plan to encourage the team to generate superior investment returns. A successful team has both the skills and the disciplined drive toward the summit, as well as a shared culture that will be needed at various points on the climb.

Every expedition team is different. The CIO is likely to have climbed to various summits during her career and brings the experience of both successful and failed attempts into the role of expedition leader. Ideally, teams are diverse in terms of background, experience, and specific skills. The terrain each has climbed is likely to provide useful insights and form

---

[1] McCullough, son of the award-winning historian David McCullough Sr., advised the students to seize the future by doing what they love, rather than taking a job for money. Wellesley High School in Massachusetts commencement speech in 2012, https://www.washingtonpost.com/blogs/answer-sheet/post/commencement-speaker-blasts-students/2012/06/08/gJQATvF1MV_blog.html.

the basis of what they expect in signing on for the specific climb. Beyond the technical skills and mental toughness, it is also essential that there be alignment of values among the team members. It is helpful if climbing partners are well-matched in terms of pace of climbing and mood.

Alpinism and investing institutional capital are challenging and intense activities that require a specific set of skills and qualities. At a minimum, the expedition needs to be a group of individuals with excellent investing skills in different areas (financial modeling, statistical analysis, due diligence, interpersonal skills, etc.). Successful alpinists and investors must have the mental fitness to endure long periods of intense activity at high levels of stress, as well as the willingness to admit mistakes quickly. The ability to remain focused and calm in the face of adversity is part of what makes a successful investor, as is the ability to mute excitement and avoid overconfidence. Being able to navigate difficult terrain in adverse conditions is required for the team to push forward. Equally important is the ability to assess and manage risks effectively, as well as make informed decisions about when to move forward and when it makes sense to turn back. The interpersonal skills required are the ability to work effectively with others, communicate clearly, and support each other in difficult situations.

Team Culture

Leaders set the tone for the team, and their actions reinforce culture. The responsibility for creating and deepening the team's culture falls to every member of the senior team, since it is in their actions and words that the culture is evident. The team knows and connects the principles and process with the practices of the team. A successful leader minimizes the gaps between culture and strategy, between values and behavior, and between behavior and practices. Culture is a system the team builds one step at a time, and it evolves as new team members are added along the way.

There are three components that underpin the culture of the Hewlett investment team. They are trust, transparency, and curiosity.

- Trust: Forming bonds of trust among all members of the investment team is critical in keeping the team safe in alpinism. Overcoming challenges, creatively finding solutions to a change in the environment, or helping team members during a difficult stretch are opportunities for ties to strengthen and interdependence to deepen.

- Transparency: Setting expectations is useful in creating trust. Transparency in decision making is essential in building and maintaining trust. Creating an environment where members of the team feel safe to make mistakes and openly discuss them is critical. Being willing to make and admit mistakes openly sets an example for other team members and provides them with an opportunity to step up.

- Curiosity: Learning by observing the actions of others and questioning decisions made along the path usually deepens skill sets across the team. We learn from each other, from what we hear from our partners, and how we are each experiencing the world around us to assess the situation and more confidently achieve our goal.

It is natural that there are changes along the ascent to the summit as members of the team decide to join different teams or take on the next challenge in their career. Successful CIOs must be attentive to changes in the mental state and focus of each member of the team to ensure the team can progress without placing anyone – or the portfolio – at risk. Team members have a responsibility to watch out for each other. To do this well, it helps if there is an awareness by the team of what motivates each team member and how they manage stress and technical challenges.

Team Structure

Investment teams are structured in one of three ways: (1) roles specializing in specific asset classes, (2) generalist roles, and (3) a combination of both. There is no correct model, and, importantly, the structure can morph over time given the specific needs and resources of the institution.

1. Specialist model: Institutions using this model vary greatly in size and tenure of the team. Typically, the CIO has two to five senior directors that serve as the leaders of investments in private assets, public equity, and hedge funds. The advantage of specialist asset class leaders is the consistency of relationship between the senior specialists and the GPs. The team also benefits from having someone who has watched the manager for many years and can access layers of the firm's professionals. In this model, the asset class leads have dedicated teams of principals, associates, and analysts to support their work. The drawback to this model is that collaboration among the various asset class teams requires intentional communication.

2. Generalist model: Institutions employing the generalist model are typically in the first five years of a new institutional investment program. Everyone on the team works on new investment opportunities, and due diligence is assigned based on capacity instead of specialty in a specific asset class. The advantage is that resources are efficiently allocated and the team learns to set the hurdle for investments as a collective result of their shared experience. The drawback of this model is the lack of consistency in the relationship with the GP.

3. Combination model: Some institutions with mature portfolios have adopted a combination model where the senior members of the team are specialists in one or more asset classes, and the asset class leads have a shared pool of principals, associates, and analysts for support. At a few institutions senior members of the team are generalists and junior team members specialize. The combination model has the advantage of having the senior leaders solidify relationships with the GPs, and the rest of the team has the ability to learn from the different investment styles of the senior asset class leaders. This model functions well if there is one person charged with staffing due diligence and portfolio management responsibilities among the shared pool of resources. As with the generalist model, the younger members of the team get access to different asset classes and ways of investing, but don't necessarily get deep experience in any single asset class.

Decision-Making Process

A successful investment team is clear on how decisions are made. There are several models investment teams can adopt for making decisions: discretionary, single decision maker, consultative, or collaborative. There isn't a single decision-making process that works for every investment team. What is essential for success is that the decision-making process adopted be clearly communicated and consistently adhered to. In Table 13.1 is a summary of the four primary decision-making models.

Managing the team requires the CIO to balance between allowing each asset class lead to exercise a level of discretion, while also allowing the CIO to have confidence that every decision made has a high probability of benefiting the growth of the entire endowment. The confidence the CIO has in the recommended actions proposed by members of the team is bolstered by the commitment of the team to uphold demanding due diligence practices.

Table 13.1

Four Primary Decision-Making Models

1. Discretionary: This model gives the head of each asset class autonomy for manager selection (to the degree allowed in the delegation of authority) and portfolio construction. Sizing is at the discretion of the asset class lead based on the role in the asset class portfolio. The asset class lead has the primary relationship with GPs.
2. Single Decision Maker: In this model of decision making, the CIO makes the decision to invest, or redeem, re-up based on highly informed input from the head of the asset class. Decisions on sizing of investments by GPs are made by the CIO based on the needs of the endowment portfolio. The asset class lead has the primary relationship with GPs, and the CIO highly engaged.
3. Consultative: This model typically refers to the CIO and asset class lead arriving at a decision to invest, redeem, or re-up, and then discussing the investment with the other asset class leads. The sizing decision is made by the CIO with input from the senior team. The asset class lead has the primary relationship with GPs.
4. Collaborative: As the name implies, the entire investment team provides an opinion (sometimes formalized in votes) on the investment opportunity, and a decision on investment and sizing is made collectively. The relationship with the GP is shared.

Source: The William and Flora Hewlett Foundation.

Size and Skills of Team

Determining the size of the investment team varies based on the size of the portfolio, the type of institution, and access to talented investment professionals. Staff turnover, especially at the senior levels, carries some obvious costs (e.g., secondary sales) and less obvious costs such as the potential loss of hard-fought capacity at oversubscribed GPs. However, priorities for educational organizations might include recruiting a fairly sizable number of students within the investment office. In this case, the size of the analyst and associate pool is large and often not included in team meetings where key decisions are made.

Hewlett believes in a lean staffing model across the organization. The Hewlett investment team is lean (usually team capacity is measured by NAV/investment professionals), and we believe having a small number of excellent team members fosters greater integration of investment ideas, creativity, better communication, and enhanced portfolio performance. A small team is resource constrained, minimizing distractions and forcing effective triage of investment opportunities. We intentionally embrace moving up the mountain in smaller groups as a way to increase innovation, flexibility, and focus. Ideally, the team spends 90–95% of their time investing.

Lastly, organizations located in financial centers such as Boston, New York, and San Francisco have an advantage in recruiting staff for their investment offices. Even in the age of hybrid work, the value of having the investment team collaborating inside a single office three or four days per week is unlikely to diminish.

Judgment is a core skill of every expedition team member. Ideally, every member of the investment team is an accomplished investor. Assembling a team with diverse perspectives and backgrounds usually results in greater conviction in decisions. Excellent teams are staffed with experienced capital allocators, combined with investors that have years of experience working at investment firms. The advantage of having both LP and GP perspectives is that the team is able to delve deeper into the health of the investment firms and the operational details of portfolio companies in the portfolio.

In addition, the temperaments and skill sets among the senior leaders of the team should be complementary. One may be highly skilled at building relationships, while another excels at quantitative analysis and modeling, and yet another at discovering raw talent. The team benefits from having these areas of strength being shared across asset classes and improving decision making from an integrated approach. The junior members of the team can continually learn from observing and questioning other team members with different career experiences.

Leadership

It was absolutely imperative that we have absolute faith in our partners for these ambitious climbs.

—Greg Child, *Thin Air*[2]

In the early years, investors think there is not much to the climb beyond the physical strain and cold weather. Experienced climbers know there is much more. It is something that must be experienced to be fully understood.

First and foremost, the most successful CIOs are motivated by the privilege of being in the service of the team and the organization. The team looks to the CIO to have a vision and unlock the potential of each

---

[2] Greg Child, *Thin Air: Encounters in the Himalayas* (Mountaineers Books, 1998).

member of the team. The CIO's job is to provide psychological safety so the team believes they can succeed in identifying managers and managing relationships. The team also needs to know they can be vulnerable and accountable in the commitments they have made with GPs, trusting that the focus will be on learning from the experience.

Fostering team culture is an essential building block of open and transparent communication. The CIO trusts that every member of the team is doing excellent work and deepening relationships with the investment partners. Management of a team must be based not just on the trust the CIO has in the individuals, but also on the trust each of the members of the team has in the excellence of the work being done by the others. Every team member must commit to bring their top game every day and be willing to support each other in making difficult decisions.

Motivating the investment team requires creating a strong learning environment, fostering a positive team culture, empowering the team, and ensuring that communication and transparency are respected. The CIO is responsible for providing opportunities for learning and growth and minimizing distraction where the team could lose energy. Encouraging the team to set aside time to think strategically reinforces the learning environment and provides fresh ideas to generate superior returns for years to come. Developing each team member to bring out their superpower is one of the key responsibilities of the CIO and goes a long way toward retaining the team.

Investment teams need to attract and retain people with a variety of skill sets that adapt over time to the changes in an institutional investment portfolio. In order to develop the team into better investors, the CIO should take into account where they are in their career. In their twenties, team members are typically looking to learn as much as possible and be included in conversations. In their thirties, they want to deepen their knowledge and take the lead on some projects. In their forties, investment professionals want to contribute the knowledge gained thus far in their careers. Critical to successful team management is understanding what motivates each of the members of the team. For some it is intellectual engagement, while for others it is a sense of empowerment, and/or flexibility. Rarely is compensation a motivator of a successful investing career.

Critically, highly competitive people need to believe that they work at the best investment team so that they focus on working as a team instead of thinking about the next step in their career. Having a shared mission and shared values helps to cement the single purpose of all involved.

Several years ago, the Hewlett investment team dedicated time at an off-site to define three or four principles that describe the culture of the team. We asked how they would describe the team to new employees or new managers. We asked what they thought was unique about how we work, compared to prior employers. We asked what motivated each of them. In the end, the team agreed on four core values: integrity, intellectual curiosity, diversity of thought, and continuous learning. We agreed to ingrain these values in every action we take.

Equally important is that the team be able to challenge investment decisions. Investment frameworks are flexible by design. New information, better arguments, and data help to shape and adapt the investment process. Being open to changing my mind is part of what encourages my team to respectfully disagree or ask challenging questions in their search for the best decision possible. From a process perspective, the team has learned that we are most effective when everyone has prepared for meetings and actively contributes to the discussion.

Empowering the team means giving people the room to shine, not just in team meetings but also in front of the IC and board. Being an inspiring leader means the CIO works alongside the team to challenge biases, to use experience to probe parts of the investment process, and to ensure the quality bar for any new commitment is held at the same high level across asset classes. It does not always work. Every investor faces a cold streak. Sometimes the asset class beta has a strong headwind. The CIO's job is to bring team members back from drawdowns and ensure they do not doubt their own skills.

Every team member should trust that the CIO will provide the freedom to develop relationships and become a better investor, while making sure there is safety so that they are able to learn from an investment decision that turns out wrong. Part of mentoring is knowing that the members of the team are likely to make another ascent as part of another team in the not-so-distant future. A CIO should provide as much training as possible so that the members of the team will be able to move to new teams where they can be strong contributors.

Designing an Incentive Plan That Works

The objective of the incentive compensation plan is to be able to hire and retain the highest-quality investment professionals to the investment team and provide them with significant incentives to create value and compound wealth for the portfolio. Therefore, a well-designed incentive plan is necessary for the investment organization to thrive. There is a material risk to the investment program's success if the incentive program fails to meet the expectations of the team.

Despite the critical nature of the compensation scheme in the probability of making it to the summit, the CIO in most institutions does not have authority over the incentive plan design. The IC or the compensation committee of the institution sets the target level of total compensation relative to a specified peer group. Institutions frequently hire compensation consultants that provide data on peer group compensation to ensure that compensation packages are within the bounds of what would be considered reasonable. In many cases, the compensation committee of the institution determines that total compensation targets a specific percentile range of the peer group.

The design of the performance plan must align incentives of the investment team with the institution's long-term performance and reward ideas and contributions to the investment process. Incentive plan design is almost always the responsibility of the human resources team because they are tasked with compensation management across the entire organization. That said, the CIO should work closely with the HR team and any consultants hired to ensure that the compensation and incentive plan are designed to motivate the team to achieve the long-term objectives of the organization. The plan should be refreshed every few years to ensure the peer group remains appropriate.

Consultants may try to steer the organization toward one incentive plan design over another. It is important that the CIO consider the potential consequences of adopting one design over another in terms of the signaling it could have for the team. There is no perfect design. The goal is clarity of design so that team members are not surprised when the incentive is paid.

Compensation schemes for investment professionals are composed of base pay plus incentive opportunity based on a pre-defined mix of qualitative and quantitative factors. Another important component of a plan that works is the responsibility of holding every team member accountable for their contribution to the goal over a three-year horizon. Goals should be set annually and reviewed periodically as the year progresses. There are years when one member of the team shines brightly, only to have their asset class performance lag the benchmark the following year. Clarity on the subjective elements of the plan is yet another way to build trust with the team.

At Hewlett the subjective review and feedback framework centers on four goals common to every member of the team:

- Asset class portfolio structure and characteristics
- Asset class manager selection and oversight
- Endowment portfolio collaboration
- Contribution as a collaborative team member

Every member of the Hewlett expedition team has goals specific to their role in each of the four main areas of work. What varies greatly among the team is the percentage of time and contribution they make to a given goal. The specific goals and time allocation are agreed upon by the team member, the CIO, and manager at the beginning of every fiscal year, and are posted on the shared drive for everyone to hold each other accountable. We found that having every member of the team have the same four high-level goals helps align everyone toward the same objective of reaching the summit.

Table 13.2 lists areas for the CIO to focus the conversation with the compensation consultant, the IC chair, HR, and the compensation committee on incentive plan design.

It has been my experience that team members rarely quit because of higher compensation being offered on another team. Instead, compensation is considered a strong signal of how much the organization and the CIO value the contribution of the team member to achieving the objective of the investment program. Empowering the team, providing ample opportunity for learning, and maintaining a positive culture should be considered best practice for anyone managing investment professionals.

Table 13.2

Compensation
• Determining the peer group for benchmarking compensation (asset size, complexity)
• Determining the compensation philosophy (percentile range of peer group)
• Time horizon for measurement of performance
• Asset class performance or total endowment performance
• Split between quantitative and qualitative incentive compensation
• Multiplier of base salary eligible to be earned as incentive
• Target range of outperformance to earn the incentive
• Any deferral component and whether deferral earns the return of the endowment portfolio

Source: The William and Flora Hewlett Foundation.

Performance Review

Creating a learning environment includes providing opportunities for team members to grow and develop as investors and as members of a collaborative team. Cultivating highly competitive and engaged staff entails honest conversations that may be uncomfortable, but necessary to make them excellent investors. There are many software systems used by HR teams to conduct performance reviews. Whether the review uses established software or not, there are other forms of soliciting feedback that many investment team members are likely to find helpful in their career development.

The performance review process should be designed to assure the IC and board that the investment team is being held accountable for the authority and responsibility delegated to them. Some institutions may require a significant amount of documentation, while others may be satisfied with a verbal conversation once a year. Again, there is no one way to conduct performance reviews because the culture of the investment team is likely to dictate the skills and qualities that are valued by the CIO and the institution.

The Hewlett review system is intended to create strong alignment, encourage teamwork, and motivate excellent work. Each team member receives a one-page written formal review every year to provide feedback highlighting three or four areas of significant contribution and two or three areas for them to work on the subsequent year. In an effort to make the review process meaningful, the CIO and manager take into account several components that provide insight into technical strengths and soft skills:

- A person's written progress toward goals
- The manager/CIO's summary of the individual's contribution toward the team's four goals
- Feedback from several GPs
- Feedback from peers (team and broader organization)

It takes time and courage to provide feedback that has the possibility of helping team members develop into excellent alpinists. As expedition leaders, we owe it to the expedition team, the organization, and the broader universe of alpinists to mentor and help every alpinist we have the honor to climb with on our expedition.

14

Managing Up

The way up to the top of the mountain is always longer than you think. Don't fool yourself, the moment will arrive when what seemed so near is still very far.

—Paulo Coelho[1]

An expedition team is understandably focused on reaching the summit and achieving the objective. Likewise, the investment team is focused on achieving the investment objective of compounding returns over time and delivering the funding the organization relies upon to achieve its goals. In the moments when the climb does not go as planned, the communication with the IC, board, and staff are crucial to the success of the investment program.

Managing up is about providing the IC and board with the assurance and tangible data that deepens confidence in the work of the investment team. The IC is part of the expedition team and needs to be treated as such. It is to everyone's benefit to invite the IC's views on potential strategic areas of focus before the team has formulated a view. At Hewlett we call these sessions Strategic Topics. The investment team

---

[1] Paulo Coelho, "Manual for Climbing Mountains: Paulo Coelho Stories & Reflections" (2017), https://paulocoelhoblog.com/2017/02/#:~:text=H%5D%20Be%20prepared%20to%20climb,is%20not%20really%20a%20problem.

prepares a report, both as a forcing mechanism for learning about a topic and to provide the IC with material so they can actively engage at the IC meeting.

Every IC and board are different. Some IC members appreciate having every investment proposal fully vetted, with no stone left unturned, before it is discussed at the IC meeting. Other IC members enjoy engaging with the CIO and investment team on ideas and perhaps are comfortable doing so only when ideas are presented at an earlier stage. The important element to note is that the CIO needs to observe and figure out what the preferences of the IC and board are and adapt the interaction and materials to their needs.

The partnership between the CIO and the IC chair is strengthened by frequent communication outside of IC meetings. The external advisors and the investment team are more effective when they are encouraged to reach out to each other between meetings to discuss specific asset class issues. The team may want to move forward without listening to the IC; however, it does so at their peril. It is important for the investment team to remember that the IC and board are equally vested in achieving the objective for the organization.

Developing Trust with the Board

There are two key elements to developing trust and managing the relationship with the organization's IC and board. The first is listening, and the second is transparency. Periods of volatility are typically when the CIO needs to actively listen to the concerns of the organization. Demonstrating sound judgment and instilling calm in the face of adversity generally improves the relationship and generates greater comfort for delegation of authority. Periods of uncertainty are also when the board and CEO of the organization need to trust that the CIO and the team have the skills and resiliency and courage to overcome challenges resulting from changes in financial markets.

Healthy collaboration on the long-term vision of the investment program fosters creativity and trust over time. It is important to the institution that the CIO consider their commitment to the institution in a minimum of 5- to 10-year increments. The commitment to provide stability in the investment program facilitates planning transitions of other members of the organization's senior leadership team, as well as the natural rotation of IC and board members.

There are moments in every expedition when it seems that there is no hope of reaching the summit. The setbacks in returns or changes in the needs of the institution can seem overwhelming. In these moments, the job of the CIO is to listen to the fears and despair, and then encourage the team, the IC, and the board to get back to the plan and head out for a new day. The optimism has to be authentic and has to be rooted in the realistic expectation that progress will be slow and that at times, the team will barely make a dent against the mountain.

In early March 2020, very few people realized the enormity that Covid-19 would become. The Hewlett team assumed we would be back to our normal lives within a couple months. The correction in the financial markets and the shut-down of the global economy seemed like enormous obstacles that would impair the ability to preserve long-term value of the Hewlett endowment. This was also a time that tested the resilience of each member of the team and the organization.

We had sufficient liquidity to fund payout for grants and expenses but had no visibility into the future. Mid-March 2020, we sat with the IC to map out a new game plan and to consult with them on potential strategies. In order to provide assurance to ourselves and the IC and board, we did an assessment of the portfolio's exposure to travel, hospitality, auto, energy, and retail. This was a moment to count what tools we had left in our packs – the food, the fuel, and even the pitons and ice screws – to assess the potential damage to the portfolio, figure out how long the foundation could sustain spending in an environment with zero visibility, and identify how to position the portfolio to take advantage of policy initiatives.

We made our team available to the foundation's staff as a resource for them to learn the impact of the pandemic on financial markets and the economy. We were transparent in our guidance and concerns, and did our part to remain calm and focused during the whiteout blizzard. Frequent updates and open communication deepened the staff's trust in the investment team. The alignment of values was essential in ensuring that an environment of trust and transparency were ingrained in every investment decision.

Transparency in Reporting

Most board members serve over a decade and rotate new members onto the board every couple of years. This results in some members of the board having greater understanding of the investment program, while others have relatively little experience or knowledge of the investment portfolio. Periodic check-ins with the board (every three years or so) to explain the objective and the risks of the investment program have the benefit of building confidence in the investment team. Board members are likely to build trust when the trade-offs between return and necessary risk are discussed in an environment that allows the CIO to be courageous and step into situations where there is little consensus.

The CIO must prove she can successfully recruit, mentor, and retain the investment team, and in many cases, be an active senior leader within the organization. The quality of the team and the investment process reflect the identity of the institution and the CIO's values. The CIO has to actively gain credibility and be someone listened to with ethics that engender trust. This process can be defined as earning the benefit of the doubt and is greatly helped if the investment team is considered "one of us" by the rest of the staff instead of outsiders of the organization.

The investment team needs to develop reporting materials based on a shared framework of understanding the objective. The materials should reinforce and remind the IC of the strategy, the long-term return expectations, and the risk involved in achieving it. The objective is to convey information to the IC, while providing details that serve to reinforce the strategy. After a successful IC meeting, the IC should have increased its confidence in the investment team's ability to successfully deliver the objective set forth.

In some organizations, the investment team forgets that the IC and board consists of busy people who do not necessarily follow financial markets closely, nor recall the strategies being deployed across the portfolio. The investment team should design materials provided to the IC as clearly and concisely as possible. Make every attempt to avoid overloading the IC with too much information. Table 14.1 offers a few tips on designing communication with the IC.

Managing meetings is challenging. It is a good practice for the CIO to work with the IC chair in developing the agenda for IC meetings. Typically, the IC chair is aware of concerns or issues at the board level that could serve as useful background in framing a conversation at the IC. If there is something that could be controversial, the CIO should make time to speak individually with each IC member to listen and learn how to craft the message in a way that incorporates concerns and validates their contribution. Regardless of how prepared the CIO and investment team are for every meeting, there will undoubtedly be a meeting where an IC or a board member may want to delve into a topic that isn't covered in

Table 14.1

Communication with the IC
• Create your materials in keeping with institutional preference, whether it is in the form of written reports or slides.
• Facilitate the IC's job as fiduciaries by placing deployment relative to policy, performance, risk, and liquidity assessment at the beginning of the materials.
• Encourage long-term thinking in every piece of communication, especially the review of performance.
• Once a year deep dives into specific asset classes are most useful when incorporating strategies, tilts, and a view on the long-term opportunity set.
• Set the stage proactively on expected returns from market beta and focus on the quality of the managers in the portfolio to generate alpha.
• Update the IC on the skills and abilities of the team in executive session (e.g., technical expertise, relationship building, strategic thinking).

Source: The William and Flora Hewlett Foundation.

the agenda. The CIO should always defer to the IC chair and follow their lead in addressing the topic.

The quality of the relationship with the IC and board determines the probability of surviving a terrible hazard. Too often, the investment team fails to consider the IC a partner and ally in reaching the summit. Board members who understand the investment program and have years of experience tend to understand the challenges inherent in managing an investment portfolio and the team. IC and board members can provide valuable guidance and defense against unpredictable ice storms.

15

Managing Relationships with Fellow Investors

It was absolutely imperative that we have absolute faith in our partners for these ambitious climbs.

—Greg Child, *Thin Air*[1]

Successful expeditions to the summit are the result of hard work and discipline. Reaching the summit is a team sport, and success largely depends on the relationships forged along the way. A smart team learns to trust alpinists who are kind enough to warn of potential challenges and works with other teams to move forward in achieving the objective. We do not climb alone, and a successful team is one that is a reliable partner to our GPs, provides insight, and helps other climbing teams to succeed.

Successful alpinists have the benefit of working alongside terrific investors from whom they can learn and gain strength for navigating rough patches. Over time they have learned to trust and observe how they build deep relationships on the mountain, how they adapt their strategies, and how they inspire their teams to achieve excellence. The more time spent talking with rest of the expedition teams, the faster the team can advance to the summit.

---

[1] Greg Child, *Thin Air: Encounters in the Himalayas* (Mountaineers Books, 1998).

Table 15.1

Characteristics of Successful Investors
• Know what edge you bring to the table and capitalize on it to maximize returns.
• Be willing to adapt and update an investment thesis or framework when faced with new information.
• Thoughtfully construct portfolios and size positions (larger positions where there is greater edge).
• Think probabilistically about the expected outcome and focus on the process.
• Have a clear grasp of financial accounting to understand how portfolio companies make money, drive profits, and be able to follow the cash flow.
• Understand the large role behavioral psychology plays in successful outcomes, and be humble.
• Understand that fundamentals can – but do not always – get reflected in the price of an asset, and know to keep fundamentals separate from expectations.
• Actively seek out learning (and reading) opportunities in fields far from finance and investing.
• Have independent thought and the courage to stand alone.
• Have discipline in evaluating each opportunity.

Source: The William and Flora Hewlett Foundation.

Every alpinist needs to remember that they are the climber/investor they are today because mentors and fellow excellent investors had the patience to walk them through every step of diligence and answer their questions. Being surrounded by excellent investors that share the same goal helps the team progress. Learning from the best investors how they balance intuition and experience with data and technical skills is what elevates every investor to be just a bit more excellent.

As every climber knows, the journey up one mountain is similar to, but unlike the journey up another mountain. There are a set of characteristics I have come to observe from having the privilege of trekking alongside some of the best investors of this generation. Each day my goal is to improve and learn from them how to be a better investor and better leader. Table 15.1 has a list of characteristics of great investors that we can all aspire to become.

Developing True Partnership with GPs

Institutional investing is first and foremost a relationship business. As an allocator of capital, we have a fiduciary responsibility to ensure that our partners are aligned with our values and will be good stewards of the endowment's capital. In order to develop trust, it is essential to understand what drives the senior leaders of the investment firm and to observe their behavior during good and bad times. Observing how they develop their next generation of investors also provides clues into how they live their values. Investing time getting to know what motivates your partners and understanding the rationale behind their strategic vision of their investment firms is well worth the effort.

We use the word "partner" intentionally (as opposed to "manager" or "investment firm") because we are aligned in our objectives and values and view them as critical to our success in ascending to the summit. Our goal is to be trusted by our partners when they think about the strategic direction of their firms or when they want to explore the broader implications of the world around them. We endeavor to earn their respect and be in a position where we are a first call for many of them, even though we are rarely their largest investors.

GPs must trust that the investment team will maintain confidentiality, beyond signing nondisclosure agreements. They trust that the investment team will not steal their ideas or worse yet, share their investment ideas with other firms. There must be trust in order to be able to openly share ideas.

At Hewlett, we sign two-page nondisclosure agreements to ensure all information provided by our investment partners remains confidential. We also do not allow any member of the investment team to trade individual securities (except the 100 most liquid stocks in the S&P 100 Index) to ensure there is never a question of whether any member of the Hewlett team benefited personally from any investment partnership. In order to remain objective in our fiduciary role, we do not allow members of the investment team to participate as investors in the funds of the GPs in the Hewlett portfolio.

Our GPs trust that we show up prepared for meetings and are engaged and present in our interactions with them. They trust that we have a long-term horizon and that we will be supportive during bad times and celebrate alongside them when things go well. Trust means we make every effort to ensure it is not a transactional relationship. The tenure of the organization's investment team is important in cementing long-term relationships. The consistency provided by seeing a familiar face at meetings and building a relationship over time, where experiences are shared over years of conversations and shared meals, is something that should not be underestimated.

I have been fortunate to concentrate my portfolio with some of the best thinkers in the world. GPs are a great source of insights into the functioning of debt markets and transaction environment. Notably, GPs are the front line in the investing world. I was a GP for 18 years and know that GPs have access to different sources of information. I show up to each of the conversations with my GPs, not from a place of seeking validation that my macro world view is correct, but from the standpoint of identifying my blind spots and gaining insight into theirs.

I have a practice of asking our managers questions, totally unprompted. For example, we may interject in meetings: "Here are a few topics; please tell us how you are thinking these topics will evolve in five years." We know that however they are thinking about the topics will be reflected in their (and our) portfolio. If suddenly, 10 managers are telling us the same thing, then we know everyone already has it in their portfolios so the ability to make money is not great, and if they are wrong, then we have a concentrated risk problem. We don't lead the witness. We ask crypto managers about biotech, venture managers about industrial companies, hedge fund managers about private investments, and nearly every manager has opinions about other asset classes.

Hewlett has a mature portfolio with an amazing group of highly experienced managers. We typically make one or two additions of new partners every couple of years, mostly to complement our existing roster or replace a partner that for some reason is no longer suited for our portfolio. Having a concentrated portfolio of partners allows for deep relationships that provide support at a business and at a personal level. The purpose of the close relationship is to have information as organizations evolve and to monitor our investments. The sharing of stories about what has worked, and what has not, allows each party to increase commitment and conviction in each other. Finally, as partners we work with GPs to develop talent within their firms. We do not share information about their talented staff and we do not try to lift talent from firms to launch them into their own firms, thereby weakening the investment firm any way.

Approaches to Diversity, Equity, and Inclusion

Hewlett's approach to improving diversity, equity, and inclusion is a fundamental part of the partnership we have with our investment managers.

It is, by now, widely recognized that our industry can and should take intentional steps to improve the diversity of our teams and portfolios. But every institution is different, and has different priorities that guide its investment program, which means different institutions may approach the challenge in different ways.

Because efforts to be more inclusive in recruitment and development began in earnest less than two decades ago and, even then, were slow to get started, there are fewer women and people of color in decision-making positions in the investment industry than expected. In recent years, large asset management firms have built successful intern and first-year programs in which at least half the participants are women and people of color. Over time, these new professionals will create a track record and then may rise internally to become investment partners or spin out with the backing of institutional investors. But investment management is (necessarily) an apprenticeship business, and it takes approximately two decades to rise through the ranks from analyst to principal/associate and from there to more senior roles. Someone following this career path will typically be given responsibility for portfolio management or investment decisions sometime between years 7 and 12. From there, to launch a firm of one's own requires taking advantage of this opportunity to establish a track record of effective decision making in both good and bad business cycles.

It is difficult to find reliable data on the state of female and minority representation in the investment field. To begin, there are no widely shared systems for tracking participation, nor uniform industry standards even for which groups to include. Some organizations that collect data include female-owned firms, while others do not; some include Asian fund managers, while others do not; and so on. Further complicating matters, investors are reluctant to disclose the composition of firm ownership, which makes it difficult to determine the extent of women and/or minority ownership. There isn't even agreement on what counts as "ownership." Many surveys define "minority-owned" as 51% owned and operated by women, Black, Latino, Native American, or Asian American investment professionals. Yet a third challenge comes from the fact that most of the data on "assets under management" by underrepresented minorities are limited to U.S.-based firms, while most endowment portfolios have a geographically diverse set of managers. Finally, measuring the role of underrepresented minorities by assets under management is complicated by the increasing concentration of assets in very large asset management firms[2]. These firms have the most well-developed recruiting and training programs, but ownership in them is highly distributed, which makes it difficult to aggregate the racial or gender diversity of the ownership base.

The Hewlett Foundation cares profoundly about diversity, equity, and inclusion, as reflected in a wide range of actions it has taken both internally and in its grant-making program. The investment team shares this concern, and we have been determined to take action that is meaningful, not just performative, in ways that are consistent with the foundation's contributions to social good. With these principles in mind, we adopted a flexible framework that utilizes the diversity of our existing investment team to help our managers develop women and people of color within their teams.

Hewlett's internal team is quite diverse, especially by comparison with our peers. Of the nine investment professionals on the Hewlett team, six are women, three Latino, and one from India. We found that building a team with greater racial, ethnic, educational, and gender backgrounds does indeed produce more robust investment decision making and top decile performance. We believe that a combination of inclusion and meritocracy is key to retaining and developing the team. Hewlett cannot compete with asset managers on compensation, but we believe that making diversity a core team value helps attract a diverse group of candidates looking for the opportunity to use their expertise to support the foundation's mission.

Unlike many of our peers, we do not approach the matter of increasing diversity among managers by focusing on minority ownership of investment firms. Due diligence and monitoring processes generally focus not on who owns the firm, but on the quality of the decision-making group within it. As such, we think efforts to promote diversity, equity, and inclusion in the investment industry should focus on increasing diversity at the decision-making table, and the primary goal should be developing skilled investment partners.

But how to do that? Given the small size of our team – which inevitably imposes constraints on staff time – we do not have the bandwidth

---

[2]According to Boston Consulting Group's study published July 2021, global assets under management ended 2020 at $103 trillion. Very large investment firms manage $69 trillion (66% of all assets) in passive equity and bond strategies. Actively managed bond and equity strategies account for $19 trillion, while alternative strategies (hedge funds, venture, private equity, real estate, etc.) represent $15 trillion.

to run an emerging-manager program. This matters, because most women- and minority-owned firms are still in the early stages of development. Given our investment approach, we expect an increasing number of these managers to come to our attention as they develop over the coming decade.

But we also want to take immediate steps to improve the situation. To that end, we focus on building relationships that empower women and minorities over the course of their professional lives. To be more specific, we have committed to taking three specific actions that leverage our team's diversity and engagement, fit the expertise of our investment team and can be taken within the scope of our regular activities.

First, we make active efforts to connect with, and help promote, women and minority investment professionals. Including a broader set of mid-level women and minority professionals in our own networks will in time enhance the pipeline for money managers' hiring plans. By building a network of professionals to whom we can serve as mentors and references (outside of their firms), we can help our managers spot talent. This is slow work – after all, it takes time to build trusted relationships – but it should produce meaningful payoffs over time.

Second, we seek to help our managers improve internal development of their female and minority mid-level investment staff. To this end, we have worked with our GPs to source mentors for mid-level women and minorities within their firms. We work directly with senior management at our GPs to organize and lead events that provide development and networking opportunities for women and underrepresented minorities in their firms. This provides the chance for mid-level staff to interact with investors to learn and network.

Our third goal is to improve the internal practices of our investment managers to be more inclusive in the selection of teams working on a deal or analysts working on a trade. This, in turn, should offer women and minority staff more frequent opportunities to gain experience analyzing and working on the kind of deals that can make up a successful track record. Only by fostering the growth path of women and minority investment professionals today can we enhance the likelihood that they will lead the firms of tomorrow.

16

Managing the Self

You cannot stay on the summit forever; you have to come down again. So why bother in the first place? Just this: What is above knows what is below, but what is below does not know what is above. One climbs, one sees. One descends, one sees no longer, but one has seen.

—René Daumal[1]

Alpinists have a love for what they do that is inspiring. It requires honesty about the reason they are attempting the ascent to the summit, and transparency as to the technical expertise they are contributing to the expedition. Most likely you have never heard of Greg Child, Andy Andrews, Lito Tejada-Flores, and other climbers, yet their adventures can inspire every investor forward.[2]

The Value of Integrity, Emotional Intelligence, and Values

My first expedition leader taught me that integrity is the most important attribute in the investment business. He was a man of his word and made

---

[1] René Daumal, *Mount Analogue: A Novel of Symbolically Authentic Non-Euclidean Adventures in Mountain Climbing* (Vincent Stuart Ltd., 1959).
[2] Greg Child, Andy Andrews, Lito Tejada-Flores, and Ed Viesturs are passionate alpinists who have been on expeditions to the most technically challenging summits in the world.

sure that every time we engaged with a partner, we were honest in our dealings and never took advantage of errors. Mistakes will be made along the way. A successful climber quickly admits a mistake and learns from mistakes to make sure the expedition team is safe. Being an investor that can be trusted to consider the safety and well-being of the team and the other climbers is critical in inspiring confidence. Other expedition teams observe the behavior of the expedition team and judge whether it is a winning team or whether the team has taken undue risk to reach this point of the summit.

Alpinists and investors are not always rational. They are driven by fear and ego, and therefore make decisions based on emotion more often than they care to admit. Being able to hold position and move forward during stressful and chaotic situations requires an investor to be unemotional and unattached to the existing plan or framework. Resilience is necessary in framing difficult moments, so the expedition team does not waste time asking why something is happening and instead searches for a practical solution. Importantly, these solutions are shared with other expedition teams in a collaborative way since we are all trying to achieve the objectives set by our respective institutions.

It is important to remember that during an expedition you will encounter many people doing things you may disagree with, or that you might find dangerous. Resist taking shortcuts. Never breach your ethics. We are called on to help others when they ask for our help. Our responsibility is to treat others with the dignity and kindness that we expect for ourselves. As climbers approach the summit, it is easy to get distracted amidst the thin and rarified air. Make sure to stay humble and keep your feet firmly planted on the ice.

Beyond the mastery of skills, being an investor requires emotional intelligence. You need to know what motivates you and what motivates your managers. Importantly, you need to define who you are in order to develop your investment philosophy. While your values are not your investment philosophy, they help to define and ground it. Think of your core values as the pillars of beliefs upon which you develop your philosophy. You are creating your personal brand based on how you demonstrate integrity, trust, expertise, commitment, transparency, and empathy.

I think of it as the three Cs of being an excellent investor and leader:

- Curiosity: You need to have a passion for learning and solving puzzles, a tenacity for digging into areas you haven't mastered, and humility to know that you never master anything because the financial markets are always going to surprise you.

- Creativity: You have to think differently. Remember that the well-worn path is unlikely to be how you learn to be an original thinker. Unless you have the ability to lift your head and understand how the real world operates, it is challenging to have the room to think differently. Generating consistently superior returns cannot occur if you are investing along with the crowd.

- Confidence: One of the surprising skills of an expert climber and investor is the confidence to climb, being sure and certain of your ability, even when there is no information or visibility, and you must take each move as it comes. It is knowing that the only way through the hazard is by climbing higher in the snowstorm and concentrating on practical solutions.

Honing the Competitive Edge

Often, I am asked to describe my competitive edge in my investing career. I usually respond that I was blessed with a gift for being able to absorb, recall, and connect a great deal of information and to step back to be able to see a contextual picture from which I can create strategic initiatives in a portfolio. This response is met with another question of "how do you learn to do that?" or, if someone within earshot knows me, they may chime in that my edge is the discipline with which I live my life and everything I set out to do. Others believe it is my investment philosophy and my ability to arrive at quick judgments. The fact is that hard work and discipline is how I sharpen and hone my intuition and competitive edge.

Investment Philosophy

My investment philosophy to risk-adjust every investment opportunity came from my years of investing in credit and emerging markets. I am by nature an optimist, look for opportunities to generate returns, and imagine the upside. To stay disciplined, throughout my career I have created frameworks that force me to consider the downside risk, not just interim volatility in the price of an asset, but the probability of permanent loss of capital.

Being flexible and adapting quickly became one of the most essential parts of my investment philosophy. Approaching the world with curiosity and willingness to listen to others around me opened many opportunities to understand how other market participants think. By keeping an open mind, I have avoided making many mistakes and have had the chance to invest in areas that I had not previously considered.

Compounding Knowledge

The best way to accumulate knowledge is to read and ask questions. When I need to make decisions, I need to have the most information available already in my head. I source material from many sources (articles, podcasts, newsletters, books, annual reports, and academic research), and not just about investments. Even when there is no time to read, I make time to read and prioritize learning over other forms of leisure. Instead of scrolling through social media or absorbing mindless content, I spend 15 minutes learning about an interesting topic. Even during the period of my life when I had three kids at home, I had to get creative. While they did homework, I would sit and read, even if only for short periods at a time. Grabbing a pen and writing key learnings inside the front cover of a book or, more recently, in the notes app on my phone became part of my routine. As my kids got older, sometimes the 15 minutes became an opportunity to learn about a topic together. Being able to explain concepts to the kids reinforced my learning. The more you read and recall the learnings from the material you expose yourself to, the more you hone your competitive edge.

Connecting Dots

Connecting dots is the art of taking a significant number of seemingly random pieces of information, sourced from obvious and nontraditional sources, and finding connections that could impact outcomes. This skill is honed over time, and unfortunately I don't think it can be taught. Some people think in contextual, abstract ideas, while others think in linear, rational ways. The power comes in the combination of both.

My obsession with connecting dots started when I was a kid. As the youngest of five sisters, everyone was busy and so every time I was curious and asked "Why?," I had to go figure it out myself. The better I got at researching everything around me as a kid, the better I got at connecting how everything was related.

In my last year of college, one of my economics professors recognized that my brain was able to consistently make nonobvious connections between seemingly unrelated topics to generate new ideas and solutions to investment problems. At this point, I had no idea what a credit analyst was, but she opened my eyes to a career path where she was confident someone with my skill set would thrive.

Upon graduating, I started working as a credit analyst, studying closely the fundamentals of corporations issuing debt and assessing whether they would be able to make interest payments and eventually repay the debt. The technical analytical skills were important to determine short-term probability of payment. But to have confidence that the company could pay back the debt in 7–10 years, my analysis had to include the momentum of the company within its sector, how it interacted with competitors and customers, and whether new companies could impair the company's ability to generate cash flow in the future. My ability to synthesize information quickly to arrive at a decision propelled my career.

The purpose of connecting dots is to be able to visualize something that is not obvious to financial markets. Connecting dots became the practice of figuring out what a company could become in 5–10 years' time, and not focusing my investment decision of what was directly in front of me.

By identifying possible scenarios of where the market may move in the future, you can position the portfolio to benefit from the development in future years. Connecting dots can generate ideas for investing in sectors or portfolio companies across every asset class. I call it "looking around corners" when referring to being able to anticipate potential hazards and "skating to where the puck will go" when describing the ability to adapt the portfolio in anticipation of a secular shift. These are skills we seek out in selecting managers in the Hewlett portfolio.

What is equally important in connecting dots is intellectual curiosity and being able to consume vast amounts of information efficiently. The network of investors, economists, strategists, company CEOs, government officials, philanthropists, innovators, and educators I have weaved together over my career continues to provide me with different ways of looking at the world. Listening to the latest areas of concern and of exciting developments in their fields provides me with a bird's eye view of how the context in which we invest is changing. Making connections with local entrepreneurs, taxi drivers, and shopkeepers provides a real-world perspective that is hard to obtain while you're staring at a screen.

It isn't enough to collect data. The competitive edge is the ability to synthesize and make judgments on the potential impact on the portfolio or a potential area for investment. You need to remove yourself and step back to see the quantum changes. As large language models (LLMs) are trained to analyze vast amounts of data in capital markets, perhaps the edge in gathering data will erode, but the judgment call will remain valuable. Until then, I will continue to learn and absorb as much information as possible to improve as an investor each day.

I spend a lot of time on airplanes flying to meet managers in our portfolio and people in my network. My team laughs that many of the best strategies we have implemented in the portfolio have come after long flights. Maybe it is the air at 40,000 feet that makes the thoughts inside my brain ping against each other, or maybe it is the white noise of the engines. Whatever it may be, the external sourcing of information and ideas, combined with the information and ideas from the investment team, has been a powerful source of superior investment returns.

Discipline

To attempt to make it to the summit in the institutional investing world requires discipline. The commitment to the craft of investing or alpinism is extreme, and the joy of my career has been finding kindred spirits in fellow climbers, since only climbers at this altitude understand what it has taken to achieve these heights. Early on in my teenage years, I developed the habit of creating five-year plans and putting them in writing to be able to communicate where I wanted to head and get support from family and friends.

Five-year plans are a useful way to imagine where you want to be in the near future. Similar to alpinism, you have to imagine how you will make it to the next ridge and the skills and tools you need to make sure you get there safely. Five-year plans are a place to challenge yourself to grow as an investor, and as a person. These plans are not straitjackets; they are not meant to be limiting. Life happens, and you adjust plans. Yet, having a written plan tends to serve the same essential role as a climbing rope and harness do in climbing to keep you from falling off the mountain.

Finding joy in serving others and making an impact on the world is the force that drives my life. Investing the endowment for the Hewlett Foundation has given me the privilege of compounding charitable assets and providing billions of dollars of funding for grantees over nearly two decades. I love investing, and I love being in the service of Hewlett's staff, an impressive group of people dedicated to changing the world. Fortunately, investing is one vocation where success can be easily measured, and delivering consistently superior returns is tangible proof that I chose the right vocation.

I never imagined writing a book. This book came about as a project encouraged by the Hewlett IC chair, Boon Hwee Koh, and board to pull together the lessons from my years as an investment manager and allocator on different expeditions to various summits. This project allows me to give back to this generation, and the next generation of investors.

By now you know that I believe the needs and aspirations of an organization, whether it is an endowment, a family office, or a hospital system, need to be the light that guides every investment decision. This book contains helpful suggestions on how to create an investment strategy, refine skills in manager selection, size investments taking into account obvious and less obvious risks, and welcome diversity of thought among the team as a way to arrive at the right move forward.

The simple truth is that luck and timing on the mountain have a lot to do with the success of the expedition team and the ability to survive on the return home. I have been fortunate in having luck and timing in finding great mentors and fellow climbers along the way. I appreciate you for wanting to become better at your role as a fiduciary and investor. My hope is that you will keep this book on your bookshelf and refer to chapters as needed during the course of your career.

The extensive research on alpinism required for this book reinforced the view that navigating approaches to the summit and having the appropriate team and equipment is just as important when venturing up a high mountain as it is inside our offices. Alpinism and investing both require determination and dependence on others, as well as a deep-rooted love of learning new skills and investing/climbing itself. Showing respect for your team and learning from other climbers is as important as your climbing/investing skills.

As Sir Edmund Hillary said, "It's not the mountain we conquer, but ourselves."[3]

---

[3] Edmund Hillary, *View from the Summit: The Remarkable Memoir by the First Person to Conquer Everest* (Gallery Books, 2000).

Glossary

2-standard-deviation event   In a normal distribution, over 95% of expected outcomes lie within 2 standard deviations of the mean. Given that the standard deviation of returns, or volatility, is a familiar and often quoted measure, a 2-standard-deviation event can be an easy back of the envelope calculation to quantify a downside return scenario that has a 2.3% chance of occurring, implying a frequency of 1 in 40–50 years. Generally, we believe this measure understates true downside risk given skew ("fat tails").

equity beta   Equity beta is a measure that captures how correlated the volatility of a portfolio is with the equity market (MSCI World). Equity beta can be calculated by taking the ratio of a portfolio's volatility to the market's volatility, then multiplying by the correlation of the returns of the portfolio to the returns of the market.

illiquid assets   Illiquid assets are those where the Foundation cannot, per the legal documents, redeem our investment within the next three years. Generally, illiquid assets are private equity-type vehicles with a fund life exceeding three years.

maximum drawdown   We calculate maximum drawdown as the largest observed percentage loss in value, from peak to trough, over a given period using monthly returns.

Monte Carlo simulation   Monte Carlo simulations are a computational process used to approximate the probability of certain outcomes. The process involves running multiple simulations using random variables, and then measuring and tallying the results of each simulation. In our analysis, we run 100,000 simulations for each portfolio.

Sharpe Ratio   The Sharpe Ratio is a metric commonly used to measure risk-adjusted performance. The ratio is calculated by taking the average portfolio return, subtracting the risk-free rate (we use three-month T-bills), then dividing the result by the standard deviation of portfolio returns.

volatility   Volatility is a statistical measure that captures the variation in price of a security, asset class, or portfolio over time. Volatility is calculated by annualizing the standard deviation of returns over the observable interval. For us, this is generally monthly or quarterly returns. Higher volatility of returns implies a wider distribution of possible values over time.

Index

Page numbers followed by *f* and *t* refer to figures and tables, respectively.